PROJECT MANAGEMENT & POLITICS

EMBARKING ON A DANGEROUS CRITICAL PATH

DR. DARLINGTON AKAISO

COPYRIGHT

All rights reserved. Without the written permission of the publisher, no part of this book may be reproduced or used in any way (graphic, electronic and mechanical, including photocopying, recording) except for the use of brief quotes by book reviewers.

Publication data on file with National Library and Archives Canada

ISBN trade paperback 978-0-578-92072-6
ISBN: 978-0-578-92072-6

Published by Soyounique Press
www.soyounique.ca

DISCLAIMER

All the work and opinions expressed herein are those of the author alone. They do not represent the opinion of any of the establishments with which the author is associated. Hence, no other party should be attributed to any errors of the fact of any kind related to this publication.

ABOUT THE AUTHOR

Dr. Darlington Akaiso is an academic scholar. He has written numerous books on global leadership studies. For over twenty years, he has worked in risk management, resilience planning, and international development. He has also taught in various capacities at the Northeastern University, University of Manitoba, Seneca College, Trent University in Canada, and the University of the West Indies in the Caribbean. He earned his bachelor's degree in Information Technology/Informatics from York University, Toronto, Canada, his master's degree in Management Information Systems from the University of Illinois-Springfield, USA, and his doctorate in Leadership from Franklin Pierce University, New Hampshire, USA. He is also an alumnus of the Massachusetts Institute of Technology (MIT), USA, and Harvard Kennedy School, Cambridge, MA, USA.

ABOUT THE BOOK

Nigerian politicians are caught in an evil cycle, and the consequences are dire. The purpose of government should be to protect its people, but what is happening in a country where resources are so abundant, yet so wasted? As a succession of elected leaders prioritize policies, projects, and programs solely on the basis of their own personal gain, they concurrently abandon what their predecessors began, frustrating potential and prosperity that should be widespread among Nigeria's people.

In this incisive look at years of corruption and project mismanagement, Dr. Darlington Akaiso clearly outlines the problems inherent in this vicious cycle. He takes us through a myriad of examples, then provides a glimmer of hope for a solutions-based response for a better Nigeria to come.

TABLE OF CONTENT

Chapter One	1
Chapter Two	14
Chapter Three	30
Chapter Four	50
Chapter Five	80
Endnotes	91

CHAPTER ONE

Project, Policy, and Program Abandonment: Falsity of Government In Continuum In Nigeria

On the evening of Thursday, December 27th, 2018, Senator Godswill Akpabio was in Uyo giving an interview to Comfort 95.1 FM. Akpabio, the former governor of Akwa Ibom State, was a sitting lawmaker representing the Akwa Ibom North-West (Ikot Ekpene) senatorial district in the National Assembly. That same Thursday, his party was preparing to receive its presidential candidate for the 2019 general elections. The party called themselves the All Progressives Congress (APC), and would be nominating sitting President Muhammadu Buhari. Buhari was scheduled to be in Uyo, the capital of Akwa Ibom, for the kickoff of his reelection campaign the following day.

During the interview, Senator Akpabio kept listeners glued to their radio sets with his usual oratory. In his speech, he defended himself against nagging queries about leaving his post as the state's governor without completing a huge project. The Ibom Tropicana Entertainment Centre, a proposed leisure and business resort centre in Uyo, would be unfinished, and some listeners took issue with this. The former governor, however, spoke with conviction about how the government is always in flux, assuring them that the succeeding administration would have the obligation to continue to work on the project even after he stepped down. To substantiate that principle of continuous governance, Mr. Akpabio referred his listeners to Heathrow's Terminal 5 (T5) project in the United Kingdom. He emphasized that it took about 25 years to complete, and that it was done under the watch of multiple prime ministers. "There is probably no British prime minister," he stated, underlining the point that projects can sustain through regime change, "that stayed up to 25 years."

In fact, T5 took 19 years from inception to completion, with actual construction lasting nearly six.[1] It consisted of 16 separate major projects and 147 sub-projects,[2] was designed to handle 35 million passengers a year, was built within a budget of 4.3 billion GBP, and involved over 60 contractors.
As complicated as the construction of such a state-of-the-art structure can be, work passed seamlessly through each phase. The tasks moved through different hands and processes, with each team doing its part to bring the project to completion.

It remains a matter of doubt whether so a grand project as Terminal 5 could have come to fruition in Nigeria. British environment and government priorities differ from what are obtainable in the Nigerian clime, where conditions can be convoluted and continuity scarce. Given the complexity inherent in mobilization of funds, technologies, and expertise - as well as in contractual vicissitudes - the project may even have been abandoned, as was the Ajaokuta Steel Project in Kogi State. This project began in 1979 and was supposed to have been completed in 1986. After successive administrations and a lengthy stall in progress due to policy inconsistencies, however, the lofty project remains unfinished as of 2021.

The Ajaokuta Steel Project is only one of hundreds of projects in the country suffering the same fate of abandonment, conceived in the present only to fall flat during the process. In Nigeria, most politicians who find themselves in power tend to act like contractors who are awarded the opportunity to manage an institution for a specific period of time. They view their administrations as their own companies, having no relationship with the administrations of their predecessors except in rivalry or competition. Like contractors who work solely for the interests of their company, political leaders work for the interests of their administration. They prioritize policies, projects, and programs that fetch them huge gains, and their main goal seems to be scoring high political points for their own team with no concern for the developmental trajectory set by their predecessors. Worse, they often attribute the failures of past projects, programs, and policies to past leaders instead of seeing them in a wider spectrum of general failures of government as a whole.

This notion is not unique to Nigeria; it can be common in other democracies with weak government institutions that are easily influenced by individuals' biases and preferences. In Nigeria, however, the battle for popularity between past and incumbent administrations is always the crux of politicking.

If government is a continuum, then what is the underlying construct guiding its continuity? First of all, government should be understood as the authority and machinery through which the will of the people is formulated, expressed, and actualized. It could also be viewed in line with Aloy Effiong's description as being "machinery through which the state maintains its existence, carries out functions and realizes its policies and objectives."[3] Whether government derives its legitimate authority from the people or from something beyond the people, the purpose of government is to control collective direction and to protect the people.

Government is guided by the laws of the land. The law sets procedures and qualifications for occupying political offices, enabling those elected officials to have legal and legitimate authority.[4] Therefore, the authority to govern is institutionalized. This authority resides in the office that an individual fills, not in the individual per se.[5] For example, the authority of a president resides in the office of the presidency, not in an individual who happens to be the president. When that individual leaves office, the authority is transferred to the next president.[6] The same concept is applicable to the governors, legislators, judges, ministers, commissioners, law enforcement agencies, local government council executives, civil servants, heads of parastatals, and other government functionaries. No one leaves the office still possessing the authority or mandate vested in it.

In military jargon, there is the saying 'soldier come, soldier go, barrack remains.' Soldiers may die or retire or otherwise vacate the barracks, but the military structures stay. In a similar vein, government offices created by law for specific functions remain in place, but the officials within them come and go. Every office is expected to play defined roles and functions irrespective of the individual occupying it, and individuals are expected to carry out the decisions of government as statutorily spelled out for their respective offices. With public administration in place, the government should take care of itself and replace functionaries through standardized processes without discontinuity.

Government has a way of checking itself against the excesses of occupants of positions in the system. A democratic government may have three branches - the executive, legislative and judiciary - that check one another in order to strike a balance against abuse of office in what is commonly referred to as checks and balances. It shows that no one branch is bigger than the laws within which the government operates. A president or governor, for instance, would not initiate a project and then attempt to execute it without having to send an appropriations bill to legislators. It must be deliberated and given assent. Once the legislature approves such a project and its budget, it then has the statutory flavor that makes it a government project. Whether the president or a governor who proposed it stays in or leaves office, the project remains valid as the responsibility of both present and succeeding administrative dispensations. The executive branch or legislature can reverse decisions, but those are done through a preset formalized process.[7]

One striking attribute of good governance is that it hinges on continuity in policies, programs, and projects. Growth, productivity, and sustainable development of the people and their society come when they are continuously built on the structures laid down by previous administrations. In other words, the well-being of a society is created only when one administration takes over the developmental processes of its predecessors. Lack of continuity in the initiatives of the past administrations usually leads to wastage of public funds, owing to the initial allocation and mobilization of resources for the implementation of abandoned projects.

The overconcentration of attention on initiatives of the incumbent, combined with the absolute neglect of incomplete projects, programs, and policies of past administrations, can be major setbacks to the continuum expected in governance.

In Nigeria, there are a lot of projects, policies, and programs that have been discontinued or ignored as a result of changes in leadership, thus making a mockery of the oft-quoted cliché of 'government in continuum.'

Government is supposed to continue the planning and gradual execution of plans in the interest of its people, irrespective of who is at the helm. During electioneering campaigns in Nigeria, one might hear candidates emerging from the same party of the incumbents serving their last tenure, saying that a vote for them means a vote for continuity. Some politicians see continuity in government merely as a particular political party continuing to stay in power over a long period of time. They hardly see it as the ability of a government to have unity of purpose in addition to alignment of vision. It would benefit everyone if the initiatives enunciated in the past could be curated and brought to fruition.

Starting from the military era, Nigerian leaders have shown erratic attitudes toward policy, program, and project implementation. These attitudes have dealt the country a huge handicap in terms of being able to sustain development. A lot of projects have been abandoned with no hope of ever being revisited. As of 2011, the report of the Abandoned Projects Audit Commission set up by then President Goodluck Jonathan estimated that 11,886 federal government projects were abandoned in the previous 40 years.[8]

Apart from wanton abandonment of capital projects, certain policies and programs have been jibbed at as well, especially during regime changes. Nigeria has had a plethora of lofty initiatives that disappeared with the regime that proposed them. For instance, in 1975, General Yakubu Gowon brought about the National Accelerated Food Production Program Policy (NAFPP). It was shelved in 1976 for the Operation Feed the Nation (OFN) Policy initiated by Major-General Olusegun Obasanjo's regime. The democratic government of Alhaji Shehu Shagari ignored Obasanjo's OFN policy and started its own fresh Green Revolution campaign. The N52 million Zobe Dam project commissioned by Shagari in 1983 to boost agriculture was also overlooked by subsequent regimes.

The trend continued into democratic dispensations that followed military handover in 1999; change of leadership has always presented a huge risk to the implementation and completion of projects, programs, and policies. From Olusegun Obasanjo's National Economic Empowerment Development Strategy (NEEDS), to Umaru Yar'Adua's Seven-Point Agenda, to Goodluck Jonathan's Subsidy Reinvestment and Empowerment Program (SURE-P), policy discontinuity and inconsistency consistently act as stumbling blocks. The N-Power, School Feeding Program, and other social safety net programs of Muhammadu Buhari's government face similar risk of discontinuity after the end of his tenure in 2023.

Cases of abandonment of government initiatives are rife in the civilian rule. Political leaders tend to play bad politics with projects without considering the economic and social consequences upon the people. It is the common people, however, who suffer the aftereffects of project somersault. For example, in executing a new road project, farmlands where owners cultivate crops to earn a living might be appropriated in order to create space for the road. Individuals and communities lose economic lifelines like palm, coconuts, raffia palms, plantains, bananas, and cassava to land clearance for the construction. When a handful of settlements are removed to give room for the road project, it may be done so with either inadequate compensation or no compensation at all. These people often live with the hope that the new road will open their community for development. Thus, they either give up their land as a personal sacrifice or have it taken away according to the dictates of law. Once the site is cleared, the work commences, but the next phase is often abandonment.

Sadly, the discontinuation of a project that demanded sacrifices of host communities likely occurs because it was not created by the current government administration, and the incumbent doesn't want to bear the burden of nursing the brainchild of their predecessor. It therefore becomes frustrating for the host community. First, the road project was abandoned only after claiming their socio-economic livelihoods. Second, they now have to deal with the fact that the partially finished project poses an environmental threat. And finally, besides remaining an unfinished eyesore, some abandoned road projects can be quite dangerous, and in some cases, impassable.

Situations like this cause economic loss on a daily basis. Where previously there was a free flow of goods, services, and people, now there might be a bottleneck or dangerous terrain. It also becomes difficult for the host community to recover the space that was taken from them. Additionally, the abandoned project can serve as a major waste factor for the public treasury as the funds that were initially mobilized cannot be implemented properly. This leaves the government with budgetary deficits that require more taxpayers' money to augment.

Another way in which project mismanagement and abandonment causes economic hardship for citizens is when the government borrows recklessly to fund the implementation of a project. When a government insists on excessive borrowing, that borrowing can kill a local economy. How? Basically, a government is expected to service and repay that debt with revenue that it generates through taxation and allocation. If the debt stock accumulated is high, then it is natural for the government to increase the Internally Generated Revenue (IGR) to meet its debt obligations. By increasing IGR, it means skyrocketing taxes on private investments, and increased taxation across the board.

This heavy taxation, fueled by state debt, has a way of hemorrhaging the lifeblood of a local economy. For example, taxes paid by transporters alone attenuate an economy as their payments are mobbed up for the IGR and used to meet debt obligations. Assuming there are 10,000 bus and taxi drivers who pay an average of N300 per day, that could be N3 million in revenues for the economy. Could we imagine what N3 million could do to a local economy every day when it doesn't have to go to debt repayment?

Indeed, the foregoing analysis has shown us how a general taxation of businesses could disrupt capital in a third-world economy, even sending it to non-indigenous creditors. This leaves the private sector attenuated for want of capital. It is very common in Nigeria to see the government applying for loans in order to execute a project. For instance, in Akwa Ibom State, the Udom Emmanuel-led state government got an N10 billion loan from the United Bank of Africa (UBA) with an interest rate of 14.5% per annum to fund the construction of the 29 kilometer Etinan-Ndon Eyo road project. The state government awarded the contract to Wizchino Engineering Limited, a Chinese company, which might have turned out to be repatriating those borrowed funds to China. This left behind 14.5% in interest for the state to settle with the lender over the course of the amortization period. Should such a project be abandoned, settlements that were removed at the site of the project, including homes, farmland, and shops, might simply be sacrificed for nothing. The servicing of debt incurred for the project and the repayment of principal would only act as leakage of taxpayer monies, encroaching on GDP.

The discontinuity of projects, programs, and policies as a result of a change in administration always has a high economic cost. Because of the uncertainty and irregularity of priorities, foreign investors appear to be reserved about doing business in Nigeria, irrespective of the vast opportunities the country offers. Scrupulous investors identify the lack of predictable policy-making as a major disadvantage. No good investor would waste a penny where leadership is erratic and where implementation cannot be guaranteed.

Most political leaders fail to acknowledge the importance of continuity with these government initiatives. When massive projects enjoy unwavering attention - even through administrative or regime change - through the final phase of completion, they usually bring state or national pride. The Great Wall of China, for instance, is an ancient series of fences and fortifications that stretches over 13,000 miles. It is the most recognizable landmark in China and one of the most audacious projects ever undertaken, and the project took over 2,000 years to erect. With unity of purpose and zeal for continuity, the Great Wall project was executed by several dynasties and leaderships, working during their own allotted times to complete the wall in phases. Even though it was initiated around 770 BC, when the Zhou Dynasty was flourishing, monarchs in subsequent dynasties such as Qin, Wei, Sui, Tang, Song, and mighty Ming (1368-1644) saw it through. During the Ming Dynasty, the wall project was taken to historic heights, ensuring that it would stem the incursions of barbarian nomads into the vast Chinese territory.

The glory of such a massive project may not be attributed to one single individual leader, but instead brings a collective pride and glory to the entire civilization. In contrast, individual leaders in Nigeria seek to use a project for both self-glorification as well as self-aggrandizement. Every administration tends to act independently, ignoring projects that promote the image of the predecessors. They often see little or no value in fetching gains on a previously set plan.

In Nigeria, a possible way to hurt a predecessor is to put the project he initiated on hold, with no regard for how it might affect citizens. It is commonplace to have former leaders bemoaning and condemning their successors for ignoring their initiatives, sometimes in the most unconventional of places. On Saturday, December 5th, 2020, for example, a funeral service for two brothers was conducted at the Ika local government area of Akwa Ibom State. Dr. Ime Titus Okopido, a former Minister of State in the Ministry of Environment, and Mr. Ini Titus Okopido, who, until his death, was the Akwa Ibom State Chairman of the All Progressives Congress (APC) were both being honored in the service. During the funeral, the former state governor Senator Godswill Akpabio had an opportunity to make a speech. While speaking, Akpabio described government as a building block, stating that when one takes it to one level, another who succeeds takes it further. He noted that when this is not done, the society surely suffers for it.

Perhaps Akpabio was decrying the situation in respect to most of the projects and policies he enunciated as governor, which were later deemphasized by his successor, Mr. Udom Emmanuel. He did, however, make a valid point: it is Akwa Ibom taxpayers who bear the cost of unused projects after billions of dollars go down the drain. The Ibom Tropicana project, for example, resulted in the loss of vast habitable and fertile land as well as having over N120 billion sunk into it. In the five years since Akpabio left office, the project languished and has remained abandoned. This is a typical example of how Nigerian wealth has been squandered, leaving the majority of citizens to reel in poverty. That money, rather than having been splurged on a single abandoned project, could have instead been channeled into education, health, and agriculture, undoubtedly improving the standard of living for the common man.

Projects, policies, and programs continue to suffer discontinuity in Nigeria. As we will find out in Chapter Four, most of the constituency projects begun by legislators have been equally mismanaged, misappropriated, and abandoned. The inconclusive projects rarely come to completion once the representatives who initiate them leave office.

If the legislators who ought to prevent their executive counterparts from abandoning projects, policies, and programs indulge in similar wrongdoing, then the common Nigerian people are left helplessly to suffer real deprivations caused by the very people they elected to represent their collective interests. Thus, it seems that the evil cycle of abandonments is a conspiracy that is systemically engineered. It keeps the power class rich and strong while the governed stay poor and weak.

CHAPTER TWO

Core Reasons Government Fails in Continuum in Nigeria

To understand why the government fails in Nigeria, we must first understand the mentality of a typical Nigerian leader at his time of ascension. The succeeding leader, during the transition, often appears to be a disciple of Robert Greene's 1998 work The 48 Laws of Power – a book that has been described by critics as 'the psychopath's bible'.

"If you succeed a great man or have a famous parent," Greene writes, "you will have to accomplish double their achievements to outshine them. Do not get lost in their shadow, or get stuck in a past not of your own making: establish your own name and identity by changing course. Slay the overbearing father, disparage his legacy, and gain power by shining in your own way."[1]

To make his postulation more vivid, Greene cites 16th century French monarchs as examples. He writes of King Louis XIV, who built his Versailles palace in the middle of nowhere, refusing to accept the palace of his forefathers, the Louvre.[2] He made Versailles the centerpiece of his reign as well as the French mark of power, symbolizing that it was a new order, one without precedent, that he had founded.[3] Louis XIV's drive for his own identity led him to abandon the heritage that had put him in the shadows of his predecessors, and he used his new palace as a contrivance designed to eclipse his ancestral legacies.

Louis XIV, also known as the Sun King, died in 1715 after a glorious 55-year reign. He vested all hopes for the continuation of his legacy in his great grandson, Louis XV, his chosen successor. Louis XV, however, thought differently. All that mattered to him were the events of his actual time of reign; the future was out of discussion. In fact, the motto of Louis XV's reign was Après moi, le déluge. This motto translates to 'after me the flood' meaning 'let France rot after I am gone.'[4]

The high-level individualism as expressed by the aforementioned French rulers is a common trait and tendency amongst Nigerian leaders today. This individualistic drive suppresses collectivism and makes leaders compete against past and future administrations. Since completed projects serve as legacies to the leaders who sponsor them, an incumbent seeks any opportunity to either create a parallel project that overshadows the predecessor's, or to abandon altogether what the former leader initiated.

Any attempt to disparage the predecessor's legacy is fair game. If the predecessor commences a project while in office but is unable to complete it due to termination or expiration of tenure, the vengeful successor creates a reason to abandon it altogether. In Nigeria, this is common.

One example is a project begun by Gov. Otunba Adebayo Alao-Akala, intended to link the end of the Lagos-Ibadan Express Road with the Ibadan-Abeokuta Road at Apata in order to ease traffic. The project was not completed.[5] While speaking on a radio program on September 5, 2020 in Ibadan, the State Commissioner for Information, Culture, and Tourism Wasiu Olatubosun revealed that the late ex-Gov. Abiola Ajimobi, successor to Alao-Akala, had also failed to complete state health facility projects in Ogbomoso and Oyo townships, noting that Ajimobi "deliberately ignored those projects due to his hatred for his predecessor."[6]

The relationship between Otunba Adebayo Alao-Akala and Sen. Abiola Ajimobi, both ex-governors of Oyo State, was defined by hostility and tension. Alao-Akala was a retired police officer who served as governor between 2007 and 2011. As an incumbent, he sought re-election in 2011, but lost to Ajimobi. Though he ran again in 2015, once again he lost to Ajimobi. One could sense why the rivalry would fester.

Nigerian leaders see the projects they enact as their projects, not as projects for the good of the general public, and ultimately, Ajimobi abandoned the projects initiated by Alao-Akala. By doing so, he painted a picture of his predecessor's non-performance, thus burying his legacies.

If old projects speak for past leaders, then neglecting them can be a way of silencing a voice that glorifies the past. Another way to silence that voice is to co-opt credit for projects not one's own. In fact, there was a time in 2014 when Alao-Akala's Director of Public Affairs, Oludare Ogunlana, bemoaned how then-Gov. Abiola Ajimobi laid claim to Alao-Akala projects. In a statement on December 20, 2014, Ogunlala said, "Not long ago, the Gov. Ajimobi-led administration said that the Gate-Total Garden-UCH-Dandaru dualization project was his achievement when in actual fact, it was executed by the Otunba Adebayo Alao administration."[7]

Other well-known political rivals whose vendetta affected project delivery led in Ekiti State: Dr. Kayode Fayemi and Mr. Ayodele Fayose. Dr. Fayemi first emerged as governor in October 2010 after a protracted legal struggle and subsequent reversal of Segun Oni's victory by the Court of Appeal. Going into the 2014 gubernatorial election for a second term, Fayemi, who had campaigned on the platform of the All Progressives Congress (APC), was squarely challenged by Ayodele Fayose of the Peoples' Democratic Party (PDP). The campaign was rife with provocative verbal attacks and inter-party tension, with accusations and counter-accusations of violence, threats, and intimidation.[8] After Ayodele Fayose emerged as the winner, it became likely that the ongoing projects, policies and programs of his immediate predecessor would suffer. Returning as governor after Fayose's tenure expired in 2018, Kayode Fayemi stressed how Fayose had shut down the Federal Government Girls' College project Fayemi had built at his Isan Ekiti country home, though he was assured he would not cancel the Gifted College project built in Fayose's hometown.[9]

Other projects also suffered due to the negative relationship between these Ekiti leaders. One example is the building of Eyiyato Enterprises Development Centre, which the Fayemi's administration commenced in October of 2012. When The Sun visited the complex in 2018 along Ire-Ilupeju Road in Oye Local Government, the site was reportedly overgrown with weeds,[10] indicating abandonment by Fayose's administration.

Yet another project that brought Fayemi and Fayose to loggerheads was Ikogosi Resort. When Fayemi embarked on a tour of projects in November 2018, barely a month after his second swearing-in, he visited the unfinished resort and expressed disappointment over Fayose's handling of the projects he left behind in 2014. It was a disappointment, since the resort was a major tourist center in the country.[11]

"I want to express my anger with what I have seen here today," he stated. "I am really upset. You all witnessed the spate of development here in 2014, you knew the patronage this facility was enjoying. What I met here today means to me a destruction of Ekiti's heritage, destruction of our commonwealth. It was unfortunate that our government had become so careless to allow this major tourist attraction and revenue earners for Ekiti to destroy and decay…This could have been avoided if the last government had maintained the facilities therein because it involved Ekiti's money."[12]

Mr. Fayose, through his media aide Lere Olayinka, said that Mr. Fayemi was only seeking "an occasion to paint him black", implying that the investment made by Fayemi at Ikogosi Resort was a fraud.[13]

The saying 'when two elephants fight, the grass suffers' could easily be employed to describe Nigeria's condition, where the poor masses suffer the consequences of the tussling of the powerful. The constant struggles of political rivals to score political points affect their intended targets much less than the people and the future of the country as a whole, especially when one succeeds another. For instance, The Guardian reported that toward the tail end of his administration, Ekiti State governor Ayodele Fayose employed a total of 2,000 civil servants, 600 teachers, and 400 employees of the State Universal Basic Education Board (SUBEB). Another thousand were injected into the Ministry of Establishment.[14] When Kayode Fayemi was elected in his place in 2018, he fired them all.[15]

When Fayemi removed his predecessor's employees from civil service, it may have been a way of avenging a similar act: Fayose had allegedly sacked some of those employed during Fayemi's first tenure from 2010 to 2014. This was confirmed by Ekiti State's Commissioner for Information, Muyiwa Olumilua, during a press conference in Ado-Ekiti on May 15, 2019.

These political leaders, in their pugnacious struggle for identity, refused to mind the law as they snatched jobs from their people even when workers' employment had statutory favor. Another instance occurred in Akwa Ibom State, where Godswill Akpabio's administration extended an Offer of Appointment Letter into Pensionable Establishment to about 5,000 applicants. This offer was in line with Chapter 2 of the Akwa Ibom State Public Service Rule (2010 edition). The recipients were to be employed as Master/Mistress Grade II, on Salary Grade Level 08, Step 2, and were subsequently issued Letters of Appointment on April 15, 2015, in effect from April 1 of that year. Nevertheless, on October 30, 2016, while new teachers were still awaiting deployment, Mr. Udom Emmanuel announced the nullification of those 5,000 jobs. Mrs. Ekereobong Akpan, Head of Service, carried it out, acting in accordance with the directive of Godswill Akpabio's successor.

How can a job that comes with security and is bound by the law of the land so easily be invalidated by the incumbent administrator, simply because it began in the preceding administration? It is not a stretch to see why leaders do this without having to take a legal course of action. This is a cause for concern, however, and it begs the question: Do Nigerian leaders sincerely see government as existing in continuum? It is bewildering that a succeeding leader would see a predecessors' projects as "his" projects. Calling those same projects "my" projects seemingly just doesn't sit right, but it can lead to a predecessor decrying it when a successor abandons what he called "his own" projects. The truth is that by individualizing these projects instead of collectivizing them, the possibility of seeing initiatives as "our" projects is automatically ruled out.

Indeed, most incumbent leaders know that one way of setting a predecessor on edge is to alter what he would deem his legacy projects. In fact, former Imo State governor Rochas Okorocha appealed to his successor on December 20, 2020, requesting that Gov. Hope Uzodinma stop demolishing "his" legacy projects, which were being overseen during his eight-year administration.[15] Regardless, two days later Uzodinma deployed bulldozers to demolish the Orlu-Assumpta Road Roundabout, which Okorocha had constructed during his tenure to ease traffic.

Okorocha also lamented that his successor pulled down the Akanu Ibiam Tunnel, constructed from 2011 to 2019. According to a statement issued by his Special Adviser on Media, Sam Onwuemeodo, "It has become necessary to appeal to Gov. Uzodinma to stop demolishing Okorocha's projects."[16] Gov. Uzodinma countered, explaining to Imo people that he was demolishing some of the structures to rebuild them up to standard.[17] It was a position Okorocha strongly rejected.[18]

Because they do not see continuity from the past to the present, succeeding leaders fail to take responsibility for the government's past actions and inactions. In Delta State during the PDP campaign, the incumbent governor Arthur Ifeanyi Okowa reportedly directed the people to blame the previous administration, led by Dr. Emmanuel Uduaghan, for its failure to complete the Trans-Warri/Ode-Itsekiri road in Warri South Local Government Area.[19] According to the incumbent governor, "You don't have to blame me that the Trans-Warri/Ode-Itsekiri road is not completed. Blame the immediate past administration and not me."[20]

These leaders fail to take responsibility for situations that preceded them in office. Perhaps it did not occur to Okowa that the authority of a governor resides in the office of the governor. It is the office in which the authority resides, not in the individual, and no one leaves the office with the responsibility of a governor and the authority to finish what was started. It behooves the incumbent to take responsibility for every project, program, and policy created and maintained by the office of a governor, whether past or present.

Projects embarked upon by Okorocha of Imo State and Uduaghan of Delta State were not their own, but were generated on behalf of the government for their respective peoples. It therefore becomes inappropriate for the incumbents to discriminate against initiatives undertaken by their predecessors.

Another core reason that the projects, programs, and policies crumble spurs from the transition of power from one political party to another. Because parties need votes to be in power, it is likely that constituencies who cast the majority of ballots in favor of the victorious party are more greatly rewarded than those who voted for other parties. The winners of the elections likely consider projects, programs, and policies that favor the constituents who gave them a majority of votes, and might ignore the ongoing projects in areas encompassing voters for other parties. In fact, in his inaugural speech on May 29, 2015, President Muhammadu Buhari promised Nigerians that he belonged to everybody and belonged to nobody. Later, however, Olu Fasan quoted him in his State of the Nation column in the newspaper Vanguard: "constituencies that gave me 97 percent cannot in all honesty be treated equally, on some issues, with constituencies that gave me five percent."[21]

This assertion could explain why some projects - located in the constituencies that gave meager votes to Buhari and APC - are overlooked while priority is shifted to areas that voted overwhelmingly for him and his party. Corroborating this position, the secretary to the APC National Caretaker Committee and a board member of the Nigerian Port Authority (NPA), Sen. John Akpanudoedeghe, was questioned by a journalist during his November 2020 tour to the Akwa Ibom State Council of Nigerian Union of Journalists (NUJ) in Uyo. When asked why the APC-led federal government abandoned the Calabar-Itu highway project, he confessed that most of the time, political office holders concentrate on working in areas that gave them more votes. They often blame this on scarce resources. In his words, "I don't want to lie because I want to defend government. I would have loved the Calabar-Itu to be dualized, but in politics there have been forces pulling government off attention. Sometimes they (political office holders) would rate based on the kind of votes they got in this area. That's politics. They would say let me go to where I had my votes. This is because of the scarce resources; and how to allocate these resources."[22]

The Calabar-Itu road project now serves as a death trap despite profuse promises by the federal government to execute the project. It's the only major land route that connects Akwa Ibom and the Cross River States, and it stands abandoned.

One thing to remember is that the two states in question overwhelmingly voted for the PDP candidates, Dr. Goodluck Jonathan and Alhaji Atiku Abubakar, during the presidential elections in 2015 and 2019. This left Muhammadu Buhari with a meager count. Take a look at the table below:

Year 2015
Akwa Ibom State

Party	Candidate	Votes
APC	Buhari	58,411
PDP	Jonathan	953,304

Cross River State

Party	Candidate	Votes
APC	Buhari	28,368
PDP	Jonathan	414,863

Year 2019
Akwa Ibom State

Party	Candidate	Votes
APC	Buhari	175,429
PDP	Atiku	395,832

Cross River State

Party	Candidate	Votes
APC	Buhari	117,302
PDP	Atiku	295,737

You can clearly see that Akwa Ibom and Cross River States gave but a small number of votes to the APC and Buhari in 2015 and 2019, though he was ultimately elected on both occasions. If the federal government under President Muhammadu Buhari abandons the Calabar-Itu Road, leaders can justify it by noting that the host states did not fully support the emergence of their party. This example clearly shows how projects, programs and policies in Nigeria are politicized, and how societal development and the welfare of the people is often sacrificed on the altar of partisan politics.

Whenever a new party takes over government, it is likely that projects and programs embarked upon by the previous administration will be overlooked or discontinued. The new party in power can award contracts to party-faithful cronies who may or may not have the know-how to execute them. It is easy to imagine them abandoned when a connection to leadership is severed.

Take the monorail project in Port Harcourt, commissioned by Chibuike Amaechi, a former governor of River State who was later appointed Minister of Transportation in Buhari's government. As governor in 2008, Amaechi initiated the monorail project, designed to cover 12 kilometers at a cost of N50 billion.[23] It was intended to make it possible to go from the old Port Harcourt to Greater Port Harcourt in 30 minutes instead of two hours, and a main goal was to alleviate constant traffic in the area.[24] The execution of the project began to scale down, however, when Amaechi defected from the PDP to the newly formed APC, following a political faceoff between himself and President Goodluck Jonathan in 2012. As the APC government led by Amaechi was handed over to Nyesom Wike of the PDP in 2015, the new administration ignored the monorail project. While speaking on national television on March 28, 2016, Wike affirmed that in spite of his administration's commitment to the completion of the projects that were abandoned by the Rotimi Amaechi administration, the monorail would not be one of them.[25] He claimed that "Rivers' people have told me not to touch the monorail project left behind by the other government."[26] The project was left incomplete.

Partisanship in a democratic setting can be a hindrance to continuity of initiatives. We can find another example of this in Imo State. After emerging as governor in 2019, Emeka Ihedioha termed his government 'PDP Rebuild Imo Administration.' The Supreme Court, however, booted his

PDP-led government in January of 2020 after only seven months in office, and Hope Uzodinma of APC took over amid many partisan prejudices. His succeeding APC administration scattered the arrangements set in place by that of Ihedioha. The Imo State chapter of PDP, in a statement released by State Publicity Secretary Ogubundu Nwadike on February 2, 2021, made it known that when the PDP Rebuild Imo Administration assumed office, they undertook massive construction, mobilizing contractors to build 25 roads across 100 kilometers of Imo State. This was in addition to more than 50 rural roads totaling 380 kilometers under construction in the World Bank Assisted Rural Access and Mobility Project (RAMP 2).[27] The party further stated that about 500 kilometers of roads were simultaneously under construction under Ihedioha, but within his first 100 days in office, Uzodinma ordered the disengagement of the contractors. This ultimately brought work on the roads to an abrupt halt[28], "a huge disservice to the people of Imo State, as the hope of getting good roads within 2020 was dashed, causing the sufferings of the people on the bad roads to continue."[29]

The Imo State chapter of PDP pointed out that by June of 2019, the PDP Rebuild Imo Administration had set the framework for the restoration of the Local Government Areas (LGAs), which granted autonomy to the local government system in the state. This fulfilled one of his cardinal election promises: setting up Interim Management Committees (IMC) for the 27 LGAs.[30] According to the party, the IMC swung into action and a "geometric increase was recorded in the economic activities of the rural areas."[31] They further disclosed their resolution that each LGA should construct a mini-stadium and an administrative secretariat, and that each LGA should construct 100 sets of 5-seaters coupled with classroom desks and seats, totaling 2,700 units and capable of seating 13,500 school children across the state.[32]

The PDP in Imo State further claimed that 27 LGAs had agreed to procure heavy-duty road construction equipment and machinery in order to complete the project.[33] They noted that the first batch of equipment and machinery arrived in Owerri at the same time the PDP Rebuild Imo administration was ousted from office,[34] stating "the local government system was restored, with life and living in the rural areas coming alive again after nearly a decade of neglect and decadence of the local government areas."[35] To the PDP's disappointment, however, Uzodinma's APC administration sent the IMC, put in place by the PDP Rebuild Imo administration, packing within its first 100 days. All this while construction of the 27 mini-stadia and 27 administrative secretariats fell to abandonment.[36] It seems that there was no way Uzodinma could have continued developing the state on the structures and roadmap set up by the rival PDP.

Differences in the orientations of political parties can constitute major setbacks to continuity of governance. A political party's ideological constructs at the helm of its power determine the outlook of democracy, and parties are judged progressive or conservative depending on the way they conduct their policies and how they influence society and the governed. And although the line dividing progressivism and conservatism may be blurred in Nigeria, there is no guarantee that PDP will continue the progressive programs of the APC.
In one example, Muhammadu Buhari's APC-led federal government initiated a social safety net program to address unemployment, setting up an N-Power Job creation scheme aimed at providing jobs for about 500,000 unemployed young

graduates. Had the PDP presidential candidate, Alhaji Atiku Abubakar, won the election in 2019, there is a high probability that he would not have continued the program because it doesn't seem to align with the PDP's conservatism. In fact, Abubakar reportedly criticized Buhari over the N-Power program. He was quoted as saying, "Even this thing they are doing, called N-Power, is a product of their poverty mindset. Nigerians do not need handout. Nigerians need a leg up! Our people are not lazy."[37]

Unlike what it might be under dictatorship or authoritarianism, Nigeria's presidential democratic system has failed to promote continuity of government's projects, programs, and policies. With the fixed tenure for leaders, the presidential system appears unsupportive of long-term planning, thus conditioning leaders to complete their plans within the lifecycle of their administration. As one government administration expires and another comes in, the chance that they will reverse the previous administration's initiatives is far too high.

The next reason Nigeria is dotted with abandoned projects is contract splitting. Despite the Public Procurement Act (PPA), passed by the National Assembly in 2007 in order to regulate processes for awarding and implementing all procurement contracts in the federal government, contract splitting still holds sway under the current procurement regime. This enables officials to evade monetary thresholds. With contract splitting, the challenge of managing projects and resources becomes more complicated as government officials split contracts to reward relatives and friends, people who might end up abandoning the projects when the administration is no longer in power.

The Minister of Niger Delta Affairs Sen. Godswill Akpabio provided an example of contract splitting on July 20, 2020. He said that successive managements of Niger Delta Development Commission (NDDC) had awarded multi-billion naira contracts through contract splitting in order to evade the minister's approval. Akpabio further explained to the panel that the NDDC management employed that strategy in order to go below the minister's approval of N1 billion. It was noted that because of contract splitting, a minister could remain in the ministry for four years without knowing what was going on within the agency.[38]

It is even possible for sub-contractors to vanish with portions of their own split contracts with the supervising ministry of NDDC none the wiser. Regarding this, one report has revealed that 22 projects were duplicated, plus mobilization fee payments of about N63.6 billion were assessed on a significant number of projects. The projects were worth about N284.9 billion, and were ultimately abandoned by contractors.[39] As of October 2019, Sen. Akpabio told Nigeria Television Authority (NTA) that 12,000 projects lie abandoned across the nine oil producing states of the Niger Delta, blaming corrupt people who treated NDDC like an automated teller machine for the abandonments.[40]

Other reasons for the abandonment of projects in Nigeria include incorrect cost estimation, insufficient knowledge of job requirements, community crises, insurgency, issues in compensation, and demands of the host community. Additionally, corruption and imprudent financial management by the contractors also serve as valid reasons for project abandonment. Since projects are often conceived by leaders as conduits for siphoning funds to their private pockets, it is difficult for any proposed project to see completion.

CHAPTER THREE

Selected Conversations On Discontinuity In Executive Projects, Policies And Programs

Nigerians seem to be hardworking and happy people despite poor infrastructure and a tough economic situation, both induced by bad governance. Oftentimes the common people in Nigeria focus solely on their own private businesses, while ignoring the gross irresponsibility of those in government. The vast majority are indifferent to government policies unless they directly impinge upon their businesses and private lives. While policies regarding the price of petrol, electricity, tariffs, and lack of compensation or other entitlement payments might draw the temporary ire of Nigerians, they soon become complacent, find a way out, and go about their normal business.

Nigerian people hardly come out en masse to question their leaders on how they spend taxpayer money. Indeed, it is rare to see protests against the lack of government accountability, corruption, and bad governance, with the exception of the #EndSARS protest against police brutality. These poor Nigerians continue to suffer economic hardship, unemployment, and lack of opportunities aggravated by officials' culture of abandonment of projects, programs, and policies. Perhaps if any of the people-oriented initiatives were completed, they could generate a plethora of opportunities and lift a majority of Nigerians out of poverty and economic hardship.

A lot of projects, programs, and policies abandoned by government in Nigeria have caused a spike in the number of unemployed youths in the country. According to a statistic released by BudgIT, "Nigeria's youth unemployment rose from 3.08m in 2014 to 13.14m as at Q3 2018."[1] BudgIT, a civic organization that seeks to help Nigerian citizens understand the public budget and implementation levels, says that when adding under-employment to the tally, "Nigeria has 24 million youths who are either unemployed or under-employed."[2] They also stress that "every year, this number grows as more and more graduates end up in the labor market, faced with a world unprepared for them."[3]

It is important to note that the poverty throughout Nigeria is directly connected to the wanton abandonment of projects in the country. Without government volte-face on these thoughtfully conceived but rarely executed critical projects, many more people could be gainfully employed and more self-sufficient. They could better be able to care for their loved ones, and society as a whole could be more satisfied and better equipped. Huge sums of taxpayer money have been sunk into projects that will never be useful if they continue to serve as a conduit through which resources are wasted.

$16 Billion Power Project

Lack of electricity seems to worsen the unemployment situation in Nigeria, and the epileptic power supply has often been highlighted as an albatross to the growth of businesses. Investors spend their hard-earned income purchasing fuel to power plants in order to generate the necessary electricity. Money wasted on power encroaches on funds set aside for salaries, and the loss thus contributes to downsizing and the saturation of the labor market. Individuals, too, have borne a heavy load caused by lack of electricity. These individuals must often resort to alternative means of energy at a very high cost.

Nigerians briefly believed that relief would come when the administration of Chief Olusegun Obasanjo promised a revolution in the power sector. The Nation reported that the entire power project anchored on generation, transmission, and distribution and would cost $16 billion. The project was supposed to extend beyond the Obasanjo administration to those of Presidents Umaru Yar'Adua and Goodluck Jonathan.[4] Unfortunately for Nigeria's citizens, however, the same news outlet reported in 2019 that EFCC investigators had discovered that most of the firms that secured contracts under the power project had collected huge sums in naira and dollars but performed less than 30 percent of the work before abandoning the project.[5]

On January 31, 2008, a committee set in place by the House of Representatives formed a report looking into how much was spent on power projects: "From the oral and documentary evidence, it was clearly established that the total expenditure in the power sector during the period 1999-2007 was US $13,278,937,409.94 billion."[6] The report further speculated that "had the supplementary budget of the power sector in 2007 been implemented, the expenditure could then have been over $16 billion".[7]

Dan Agbese, a veteran Nigerian journalist and newspaper columnist, attributes part of the failure of the power project to internal government sabotage while emphasizing how Obasanjo frustrated his own initiative. He observes that "a good example of this is the purchase of eighteen gas turbines by Obasanjo. At the time he bought them, the system was not prepared to receive them because the basic things such as gas pipe lines had not been laid; nor was their housing ready for installation. The turbines spent more than one year before they were eventually cleared from the port. By this time, Obasanjo had left office. In a way, the former president sabotaged his own energy policy by buying gas turbines he knew could not be put to immediate use."[8]

Agbese also notes that some of the contractors were fully paid without even knowing where their contract sites were located, and the situation was additionally complicated by external sabotage. He reveals that the project was under the control of a powerful and vicious cabal, easily manipulated by the generator merchants and their collaborators in the public sector.[9] According to Agbese, this cabal sought to make people's dependence on generators total and permanent.[10] "An improved power generation and transmission," he explains, "threatens their source of wealth."[11]

In 2005, President Obasanjo oversaw the transformation of the National Electric Power Authority (NEPA) to the Power Holding Company of Nigeria (PHCN), unbundling the company in the process. In line with the Electric Power Sector Reform Act, the PHCN was privatized in 2013 during Goodluck Jonathan's administration and was divided into one transmitting company, six generating companies, and 11 distributing companies. Despite the effort to reform the country's electricity industry, Nigerians are still enduring insufficient power supply with perpetual power outages, a combination that leads to poor performance of businesses and a high cost of acquiring energy. In fact, Mr. Aaron Artimas, an advisor to Minister of Power Mr. Sale Mamman, disclosed in a February 2021 statement in Abuja that the federal government spends over N50 billion monthly on electricity.[12]

"Worried by the incessant complaints by ordinary Nigerians over the unavoidable and periodic increase in the cost of electricity, the Federal Government has been subsidizing electricity supply in the country to the tune of over N50 billion," said Artimas. "The funds are provided to augment the shortfall by the Distribution Companies (DiSCos) who have failed to defray the cost of bulk electricity supplied to them by the Generating Companies."[13]

This lamentation proves that the power project that gulped billions of dollars not only failed, but was an immense waste of resources and opportunities to Nigerians.

NNPC Greenfield Refineries Project

Nigeria is one of the leading net exporters of crude oil in the world. Despite oil wealth, however, the country has spent billions of dollars on the importation of refined petroleum for domestic consumption; Reuters reports spending of about $5.8 billion on fuel imports from late 2017 to February 2018.[14] Data connected to the Nigerian National Petroleum Corporation (NNPC) shows that prevailing consumption of gasoline or Premium Motor Spirit (PMS) is estimated at 35 million litres per day, while kerosene is only ten million litres per day. Here we can see that Nigeria spends between $12 and $15 billion annually in order to meet the deficit in supply.[15xxxxxx] It's hard to imagine how a seemingly oil-rich country allows such huge sums of money to fly out the window in the name of fuel exportation, leaving the domestic economy weak for want of capital.

Due to a lack of visible progress on the 18 licenses issued for private refineries since 2002, and in order to urgently increase the crude oil refining capacity within the country, it became evident that there was a need for NNPC Greenfield Refinery Projects Division (GRPD). In late 2005, the Projects Division was brought to life.[16] It was against this backdrop that the NNPC proposed one refinery each in Bayelsa, Kogi, and Lagos States in 2011 with feasibility studies fully paid for and carried out. When similar projects were proposed in Delta and Imo States in 2018, reactions varied, though the previous projects already lay abandoned. BudgIT, for instance, declared that "it is wrong for any government institution to tease citizens with announcements for Greenfield crude oil refineries, award huge sums for feasibility studies, abandon the project when it's time for construction, then repeat the cycle in another state."[17]

The way the country's leadership is showing an interest in project formulation should raise hope that the country may reap the good fruits of that labor, born of meaningful vision and careful planning. Sadly, however, all Nigeria reaps from this are more waste and mass impoverishment. As previously outlined, leaders threw bundles of money into projects that were eventually abandoned or delayed. And when processes are delayed, another round of funds is required to revive the project. This vicious and needless cycle has done serious harm to the country's economy and to its people. Timely completion of the Greenfield refineries could have instantly created employment for the teeming jobless population. It could have boosted related investments in the surroundings of the sites, and could have cut down on the splurging of taxpayer money to middlemen who feast on Crude Oil Lifting (COL) contracts. The project could also have easily removed bottlenecks that feature in the importation of fuel from foreign countries and the associated capital flights and wastages.

Ajaokuta Steel Project

Steel is a multi-functional and adaptable material that can serve as the backbone of industrialization. When Britain developed its iron and steel industries in the 19th century, the industrial revolution that followed earned the nation its 'Workshop of the World' sobriquet. If applied in Nigeria, massive steel industrialization could be a panacea to the high rate of youth unemployment. This is not currently feasible, however, due to the lack of a functional steel production complex.

Prof. Kole Omotoso, founder of the Africa Diaspora Research Group in Centurion, South Africa, affirmed that the lack of a functional steel complex anywhere in the country would make it impossible for Nigeria to achieve any meaningful technological growth before the year 2020.[18] "In 1979," he explained, "the federal Government of Nigeria under General Olusegun Obasanjo, signed a global contract that was opened to bidders from the whole world. The leaders believed then that without a functional steel industry, there can be no industrialization and no material with which to build infrastructure."[19]

The contract for the establishment of the Ajaokuta Steel Complex project was reportedly awarded in 1979 to TyajzPromExport, headquartered in what was then the Union of Soviet Socialist Republics (USSR). It was reviewed in 1986 during Ibrahim Babangida's junta, when a completion date was set for 1989. The government claimed to have spent $5 billion on the Ajaokuta Steel Complex project, when it was supposed to have cost $650 million.[20] They poured more funds into the project, but the steel complex remained at death's door. In May 2020, when the federal government inaugurated the Ajaokuta Presidential Project Implementation Team, an estimated US $1.46 billion was reportedly pledged to revamp the steel complex. The support would allegedly come from Afreximbank and the Russian Export Center.[21] This signaled that yet another round of expenses might be incurred through funding a project doomed for failure. The president, however, rejected a bill from the Senate seeking $1 billion from the Excess Crude Account that could be used to fund completion of the steel mill.[22]

The continued calls to fund this stagnant project seems suspicious. Will the funds be used wisely, or will they merely provide more opportunities for this generation's leaders to make capital gains? After all, Prof. Kole Omotoso said that the steel project is "one of the bottomless drain pipes of the national coffers."[23]

Ajaokuta Steel Complex /Photo: Aljazeera

Ibom Science Park Project

Ibom Science Park is an Akwa Ibom State project in southern Nigeria. The science park was supposed to serve as a technology hub, not only to Nigeria, but to Africa as a whole. In fact, it was touted to be the next Silicon Valley. The Akwa Ibom State government, under Arc. Obong Victor Attah, initiated the project in the hopes that it would spark job creation and grow the digital economy. It was thought that the nagging problem of youth unemployment in Akwa Ibom State could be solved by the addition of this project, since it would create a usable space for young entrepreneurs and ICT-based start-ups that could usher in an industrial revolution. The Akwa Ibom State government reportedly paid the main contractor, SBT Juul of South Africa, N5.2 billion out of the contract sum of N6 billion.[24] Unfortunately, this laudable project was abandoned after Victor Attah left office in 2007 and his successor, Godswill Akpabio, refused to continue implementation of the project.

With wide condemnation trailing him for abandoning the Ibom Science Park project, Akpabio advanced the reasonable excuse that it was impossible for his administration to continue after over 90 percent of funds distributed to the contractor who could have implemented the project through its final phase were mobilized during his predecessor's era. The Guardian quoted Akpabio's media aide, Mr. Anietie Ekong, as revealing the total cost of the project to be N5.6 billion. Ekong added that Attah's administration paid N5.3 billion upfront, while the actual work completed was worth less than N400 million.[25]

In 2009, The Akwa Ibom State House of Assembly set up a committee chaired by Uruan State constituency representative

Usen Akpabio to determine whether money paid for the project was proportional to the work completed. When the committee finalized the report, it revealed that funds released for the project made their way into the pockets of individuals rather than to contracted companies. This atrocity explains why the project was abandoned even though over 90 percent of the contract sum was paid out.[26]

According to a National Bureau of Statistics report in August 2020, the rate of unemployment in Akwa Ibom was 45.2 percent;[27] completion of the Science Park project could certainly have helped slash this. As of 2020, the state recorded the second highest percentage of unemployment in the country after Imo State. Akwa Ibom State has also consistently been the second highest recipient of allocation funds from the federation account.

As of December 2019, the government of Mr. Akpabio's successor Udom Emmanuel has made moves to complete the Science Park. During the re-launching ceremony, the project was renamed Ibom Blue Sea Science and Technology Park and is expected to be completed under the Public Private Partnership (PPP) arrangement at an estimated cost of approximately 500 million Euros. It seems like a good idea, but could this be another way of draining taxpayer money?

East-West Road

If completed, the East-West road would be one of the most economically strategic routes in Nigeria, spanning the majority of states in the Niger Delta region. This region bears most of the country's crude oil and contributes to more than 90 percent of Nigeria's foreign exchange. Despite oil wealth found in the region, however, infrastructure leaves much to be desired. Poor road networks continue to deprive the region's people of economic opportunities, since lack of free-flowing traffic hampers Niger Delta's domestic economic performance.

The story of the East-West road is another of wastages, gross project mismanagement, and corruption. The 337k road project was awarded in 2006 by President Olusegun Obasanjo's administration to four different construction companies with a completion deadline of August 2009. The road was begun, running from Effurun in Delta State to Oron at a point that borders Cross-River and Akwa Ibom States.

The project was divided into four sections and cost N211 billion. Section I is the 87k Warri to Kaiama route through Delta and Bayelsa States, and was awarded to Setraco Nigeria Limited for a total of N64.1 million. Section II, a 101k Kaiama to Port Harcourt road in Bayelsa and Rivers States, was awarded to Julius Berger PLC at N79.2 million. Port Harcourt through Eket made up section III, spanning 99k; it was awarded to Reynolds Construction Company (Nigeria) Limited at a cost of N35.6 million. The last division of the project, section IV, a 50k stretch from Eket to Oron Road in Akwa Ibom State, was awarded to Gitto Costruzioni Generali Nigeria Limited for a bid of N26 million. When militant activities in the Niger Delta region reportedly forced Julius Berger PLC to abandon section II, it was re-awarded to Setraco Nigeria Limited.[28]

There was change, however, in management as the supervision of the highway project was removed from the Ministry of Works and given to the Ministry of Niger Delta Affairs in

2009. According to a Vanguard report, "The cost of the project which was first awarded in 2006 for a combined sum of N211 billion was reportedly reviewed upward to the tune of N349.8 billion."[29]

In August of 2020, the Minister of Niger Delta Affairs, Sen. Godswill Akpabio promised that the four sections of highway projects would be completed by December 2021, as President Mohammadu Buhari's government had decided to revisit the project. But a few months later, The Guardian reported Akpabio's claim that completing the East-West road would ultimately consume about N1 trillion.[30] To this end, the failure of the East-West road project has exposed Nigeria's deficiency in project management and the associated risk mismanagement culture. A project that was budgeted at an initial cost of N211 billion would now be N1 trillion; the proposed completion date of 2009 was pushed to 2021. The numbers are staggering and hard to believe, since a project that was slated to take four years at most would now take over 15 to be completed.

Calabar-Odukpani-Itu Road Project

The Calabar-Odukpani-Itu road appears to be the only major land route that links Cross River to Akwa Ibom and the rest of the South-South states. Two of these states, Akwa Ibom and Cross River, have long-standing commercial and sociocultural relationships along with a close economic interdependence. The land route connecting them appears to serve as a lifeblood to their interstate relations.

The road, first constructed as a single lane in the 1970s, has become deplorable in the 21st century due to excessive pressures of human and vehicular movements. It has become so unmanageable that businesses are avoiding it altogether, thus cutting the economic linkages in the region. It is so bad that simply transporting bottled products through the route can be a huge risk to everyone involved. It was so apparent that Georgios Polymenakos, managing director of Champion Breweries, cried out during an awards ceremony at the University of Uyo that his company was finding it difficult to transport its products to Cross River and other states because of its awful condition.[31]

A contract to update the road was awarded on April 24, 2018, to Julius Berger PLC at N54.1 billion. It was supposed to last for 30 months, but only 13 months after the project was awarded, Julius Berger stated that the work was suspended due to lack of funds from the government.[32] As stated earlier, Akwa Ibom and Cross River's weak political support for the ruling APC in the February 2019 presidential election may have been what prompted the APC-led government to commit the volte-face on the project.

The project had been subjected to irregularities ab initio. As a result of public outcry and hardship faced by the motorists plying the Calabar-Odukpani-Itu road, the Committee on Works and Abandoned Projects of the Akwa Ibom State House of Assembly, headed by Francis Uduyok, accompanied project contractors to the site in October of 2019 to ascertain the actual state of the road, which supposed to come with a spur at Ididep. They discovered that out of the proposed 87 kilometers, only 21.9k had been awarded for construction, and that was at a whopping sum of approximately 54 billion.[33]

The sorry state of the road has caused economic hardship and socioeconomic deprivation to the people of the region. This is evident in many ways, but one of the most striking is how it has affected citizens' access to a basic human need: food. Lack of prompt evacuation of food items from the Odukpani area, the chief supplier of food in the Akwa-Cross axis, mostly leads to food spoilage. It has become so difficult to transport these items to Akwa Ibom and beyond that these government project hold-ups have led to food scarcity and high cost of products. Abandoning this strategic road project has consequences that not only affect members of the opposition parties, but also all road users irrespective of partisan affiliation.

Abandoned Calabar-Odukpani-Itu road in deplorable state

Nuclear Centre Project

When it comes to the health of its citizens, Nigeria seems to fare badly. The country's enormous shortfall in health funding[34] has resulted in the common people dealing with serious health risks. The government appears to care little about pollution of the environment as well. Radioactive waste is highly toxic, and as the country fails to manage it, the population stays at higher risk of cancer, anemia, and genetic and cardiovascular disease. An egregious example of a failed attempt to address this follows.

The importance of nuclear power cannot be overemphasized in the modern era as the emerging nuclear reactor technologies seek to bring about low carbon energy. This causes a reduction in greenhouse emissions, improving human health that would otherwise be hampered by gaseous pollutants.

In 2009, a low-to-medium radioactive waste management project was awarded at the contract sum of N401.4 million to Commerce General Limited, and of that, N312 million was reportedly paid.[35] The online news medium Premium Times assessed that if the contract was awarded at N401.4 million, with N312 million paid so far, then the balance should have been about N89 million. On the contrary, the Nigeria Atomic Energy Commission (NAEC) quoted N329 million.[36] This outrageous figure shows how Nigeria's money is blown away on seemingly nothing, with the original goals of spending remaining largely unachieved.

Problems with project management continue to be Nigeria's Achilles' heel in every part of the process. If only Nigerian government officials involved in awarding a project to a contractor were called upon to give a truthful account of their processes, there would be some semblance of accountability. In reality, officials often simply inflate the percentage of the process that has been completed in order to make themselves look good. With some accountability measures in place, more eyes could be watching the processes as the project moves throughout its life cycle. While things would certainly be delayed sometimes, as they often are in large projects, having a keen set of eyes there would help these big projects stay on the radar rather than be abandoned altogether. A clear example showing the need for accountability is when Premium Times interviewed a NAEC official over the abandoned radioactive waste management facility. The response was that the project was not abandoned and was 78 percent complete, only suffering delays.[37] But according to the news medium, "while the commission said the project was 78 percent complete, a visit to the facility told a different story: an expanse of land overgrown with weeds and a construction no way near half-way complete which, in no way, justified the commission's claim of paying almost 80 percent of the total contract sum to the contractor."[38]

The nuclear instrumentation laboratory project at the center was reportedly abandoned as well, after the project was awarded at the cost of N829.6 million to Trois Associates Ltd in 2012. As of 2018, NAEC claims to have attained 68% of completion.[39] The laboratory was supposed to serve as workshop for students, researchers and others in the nuclear field,[40] but the culture of abandonment ruined this lofty initiative.

Abandonment Of Vision 20: 2020

Vision 20: 2020 was a grand national development plan for Nigeria. Leaders hoped it would put them in the same league as the best economies in the world by the titular year. The plan, initiated by President Olusegun Obasanjo in 2006, was taken over by Umaru Musa Yar'Adua, who assumed office in 2007. To give Vision 20: 2020 a direction that would increase the GDP to at least US$900 billion by 2020 (in comparison with 2008's US$212 billion)[41] Yar'Adua formulated and launched the Seven Point Agenda on August 1, 2007[42] with implementation strategies designed to ensure the actualization of the vision. The main body vested with the responsibility for development was the National Council on Vision 2020, chaired by the President. There was also the National Steering Committee consisting of about 70 people; the National Technical Working Group consisting of 20-25 experts in specified thematic areas; the Stakeholder Development Committee, which included state governments and federal ministries, departments and agencies (MDAs); and other key institutions.[43] With the commitment to this laudable national policy, Yar'Adua inaugurated a study group of a thousand experts working for more than nine months to produce a draft of Vision 2020. The blueprint of Vision 2020[44] was eventually launched on September 25, 2009. The accompanying agenda prioritized power and energy, food, wealth creation, transportation, land reforms, security, and education.

On the launching day of the blueprint of the Vision, Vice President Goodluck Jonathan vouched for the success of the policy: "What we are saying through this blueprint, is that we are prepared to take the necessary steps to place us in our rightful place in the committee of nations. The targets for 2020 are realistic and can be achieved even before then."[45] Unfortunately, on his presidential inauguration day on May 29, 2011, Jonathan introduced another policy called Transformation Agenda without articulating a clear-cut directive. This ushered in an era of ambiguity in policy implementation as Nigeria steadily moved toward the year 2020.

Vision 2020 was a policy of the successive Peoples Democratic Party (PDP) governments, which may explain why Muhammadu Buhari's APC-led government ignored the vision and its analogs while launching the Economic Recovery and Growth Plan (ERGP) to undo economic damages he blamed on 16 years of PDP rule. The ERGP, however, focused on achieving economic growth without actually aiming at positioning the country among the 20 biggest economies in the world.

In September of 2020, President Muhammadu Buhari inaugurated the national steering committee with co-chairs Atedo Peterside and Zainab Ahmed, Minister of Finance, Budget and National Planning. The committee was charged with overseeing the development of the Nigeria Agenda 2050 as well as the Medium-Term National Development Plan. According to President Buhari, "The main objectives of these successor plans are to lift 100 million Nigerians out of poverty within the next 10 years, particularly given the World Bank's projection that Nigeria will become the world's third most populous country by 2050 with over 400 million people."[46] This move signaled the final nail in the coffin of Vision 20: 2020.

The adoption, then abandonment of policies and programs in Nigeria could be described as one step forward and two steps back. As a result, Nigerian people have endured unbearable hardship. The country reportedly has the highest number of people living in extreme poverty in the world, with an estimated 86.9 million said to be living on less than N381 a day.[47] This is an utter contradiction to the vision hatched in 2006 to place Nigeria amongst the 20 most developed economies by 2020. Instead, as of January 2020, the country was among the top ten countries in the world in the 'misery index', and has one of Africa's highest unemployment rates with 23 percent of its population without jobs.[48]

CHAPTER FOUR

Discussion and Mini-Compendium Of Failed Constituency Projects

The worst of all forms of project mismanagement and discontinuity are found in zonal intervention projects (ZIPs), otherwise known as constituency projects. These are certain projects in the annual budget executed in legislative constituencies with the active participation of the legislators.[1] In 1999, when military rule ended and democracy rebooted in Nigeria, legislators demanded tangible evidence of democratic dividends for their constituents. The ZIP initiative was proposed to drive development to the grassroots. The leadership of the National Assembly then approached the executive arm under Olusegun Obasanjo, demanding the approval of constituency projects. According to Patrick Udefuna et al, senators initially received N5 million each, while every member of the House of Representatives received N3 million as a constituency allowance, although payments were not reflected in the budget.[2]

While Section 80 (items 2, 3 and 4) of the Constitution of the Federal Republic of Nigeria of 1999 enables the National Assembly to appropriate funds for government spending, legislators are expected to recommend projects for their constituencies based on the prevailing needs of the constituents. While a noble sentiment, Sen. Femi Okuronmu notes, "the award of contracts for, and the supervision and payments for such contracts were left completely in the hands of the appropriate executive agencies of government."[3]

It should be observed that any other project not nominated by a legislator, but appointed by a ministry or agency for a community, is simply a budget project and not a constituency project.

It was believed that by introducing this initiative, constituents would become actively involved in identifying developmental projects for implementation in their domains, thus offering opportunities for wider articulation. All in all, the concept offered ample opportunities for elected representatives to directly participate in the alleviation of the challenges faced by their constituents. Unfortunately, the running and implementation of constituency projects in Nigeria have fast become a matter of controversy. In fact, these projects often turn out to serve as pipes through which the country's resources are drained.

President Obasanjo, speaking in Abuja in 2010 at a retreat for Niger State senior civil servants, accused National Assembly members of inserting items into the budget that were not actually required to complete things. Obasanjo also alleged that they often connived with contractors in the execution of constituency projects by taking kickbacks, while further disclosing that annually, it cost the government more than N250 million per head to maintain federal lawmakers.[4] Similarly, President Muhammadu Buhari lamented in November 2019 that N1 trillion had been spent on constituency projects in ten years with no impact on the lives of the common Nigerians. In his words, "It is on record that in the past ten years, N1 trillion has been appropriated for constituency projects yet the impact of such huge spending on the lives and welfare of ordinary Nigerians can hardly be seen."[5]

Nowadays, it is common to see legislators acting as if they are carrying out constituency projects out of sheer personal benevolence to their people. In a 2016 article, Tonnie Iredia reminds us of a case in which Sen. Gbenga Kaka, a lawmaker who represented Ogun East Senatorial District, and his successor, Sen. Buruji Kashamu, engaged in a verbal war over the ownership of a constituency project in the area.[6] One accused the other of going about erecting ownership signposts at the sites of the project.[7]

It is regrettable that Nigerian lawmakers exert undue influence on various agencies of government in order to manipulate the terms of these contracts, in many cases diverting funds for projects to their own use. As Tonnie Iredia further reveals, it is no secret that some legislators are also the contractors selected to execute their nominated projects. Citing a finding of an unnamed investigation, Iredia alleges that "although constituency projects are advertised as required by law, lawmakers have devised dubious ways of ensuring that only companies fronting for them or those belonging to the cronies are pre-qualified."[8]

From the very beginning, the concept of constituency projects has been mired in controversy. Several disagreements have dominated the debate between the executive and the legislative arms of the government over the issue of inclusion of constituency projects in the budgets. On several occasions, budgets have been delayed. When the appropriation bills were eventually passed into law, there were significant differences between the estimates submitted by the executive branch and the amount eventually approved by the legislature.[9] The increase in such budgetary estimates, in several instances, came about due to insertion of numerous constituency projects. Another problematic aspect of constituency projects appears to be that inflated prices seriously encroach availability of resources.

Seeing this, BudgIT designed Tracka in 2014 as a platform to enable citizens to follow up on budgetary capital expenditure and constituency projects in their own communities. Because of an increased number of abandoned projects, Tracka was founded to track budgetary implementation and to ensure service delivery in Nigerian communities.[10]

As Tracka has exposed, the trend emerging in zonal intervention projects shows an alarming rate of irregularities. The outfit noticed that inflated costs and the overpricing of government deals are both common. According to Tracka, the unusual cost of construction in Nigeria compared with global numbers is mind-boggling.[11] In one example in Edo State, 180 million was budgeted in 2017 for skill acquisition training and empowerment in Edo North Senatorial District, but the undertaking was only partially executed.[12] In another in the same year, it was found that over N104.9 million was allocated to Enugu North Senatorial District in Enugu State for 251 motorcycles at the rate of N418,000 each.[13] This was far above the cost of a motorcycle at that time.

These examples are just the tip of the iceberg. Tracka's investigative outfit points out that lawmakers have turned themselves into the biggest beneficiaries of empowerment provisions.[14] Findings also stress that tracking empowerment has been a difficult task, as resident beneficiaries are mainly party loyalists,[15] who might not volunteer information for investigations. In March 2021, Tracka raised further alarm over the allocation of over N59 billion for ZIPs nominated by members of the National Assembly.[16]

Tracka's review of constituency projects also reveals that from 2016 to 2021, over 50 percent of projects nominated by lawmakers were empowerment projects; it also revealed that a whopping N63 billion and N59 billion were allocated for empowerment provisions in 2020 and 2021, respectively.[17]

Another concern is that a lot of constituency projects that have found their way into the budget lack specific project locations. According to Tracka, 173 line items in the 2017 ZIPs did not have proper details denoting the states, senatorial districts, or local governments where the projects would be carried out,[18] and projects with unspecified locations were reported to have gulped N1.8 billion of the 2017 budget.[19] Failing to provide these locations for transparency deprives the citizens, auditing bodies, and civil society of the opportunity to monitor the implementation of the government's dividend management.

Once a constituency project is abandoned during the tenure of a sitting lawmaker, it becomes almost impossible for the successor to retrieve allocated funds and push for completion. These projects litter the whole of Nigeria. Every year, money is allocated for interventions in various constituencies, then never accounted for. This leaves many curious about whether these projects were meant to better the lives of the common people, or to serve as a means of enriching legislators.

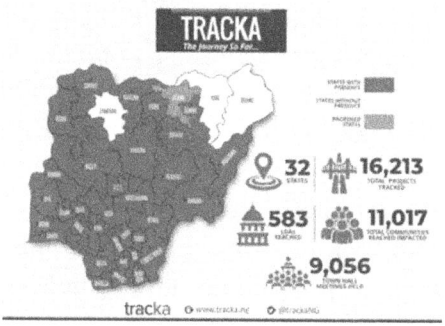

Pictogram as of the first quarter of 2021

Mini-Compendium Of Failed Constituency Projects (2017-2020)

The following are examples of projects that have failed to meet the purpose for which they were initiated. Although it would take several massive book volumes to compile and present all the failed constituency projects in the country, this mini compendium can serve as a window to the irregularities found in the management of zonal intervention projects in Nigeria.

YEAR 2017

Infrastructure Provision of Obubra National Youth Development Center

Project Location: Cross River State

Cost: N30 million (in 2016 budget), N50 million (in 2017 budget)

Located in Cross River State, this project initially cost N30 million, but the next year appeared as N50 million. On September 19, 2017, the Tracka team visited the Obubra traditional rulers' council to sensitize them on this project, since nothing was done on the site. Efforts to organize a town hall meeting were said to have been frustrated by loyalists to Sen. John Owan Enoh, who represented the district.[20]

The youth development centre, when completed, was supposed to accommodate and provide workshops for the teeming youth in Obubra Local Government Area with the skills needed to be self-employed and independent.[21]

Comprehensive Health Center, Solar Powered Borehole, and Maternity Ward

Project Location: Aniocha-Ugbo, Aniocha North LGA/Oshimili Federal Constituency

Cost: N33 million

At the time of Tracka's reporting, the health center, solar-powered borehole, and maternity ward projects were left undone in the Aniocha-Ugbo community. During Tracka's visit to the community, they learned that leaders preferred a renovation of the existing health center over constructing a new one, though the local people did cite a solar-powered borehole and a maternity ward for pregnant women as important needs.[22]

When Tracka visited the site in May of 2018, none of the projects had commenced. A phone call to Joan Mrakpor, their representative in the federal government, revealed that the project had been moved to the 2018 budget and would no longer be implemented within the budget of 2017.[23]

Sensitization and Strategic Empowerment on the Rights of People Living with HIV/AIDS

Project Location: Etsako East LGA, Edo North Senatorial District

Cost: N130 million

As of June 2018, this project had not been implemented. When Tracka's Project Tracking Officer (PTO) interacted with residents of Etsako East LGA over provisions of empowerment for people living with HIV/AIDS, they expressed displeasure over the project implementation in the previous year.[24]

Construction of Six Motorized and Eight Hand Pump Boreholes

Project Location: Ikole/Oye Federal Constituency

Cost: N60 million

In Oye-Ekiti, portable water is so scarce that residents are forced to walk for kilometers just to fetch it from streams and other untreated sources. This constituency project, which could have reduced the challenge of water scarcity, had not begun as of 2018.[25]

In March 2018, residents complained that their legislator had not responded to their queries on the water project. They also complained about the general poor state of basic amenities within the community: the dearth of good roads, schools, quality hospitals, and more. They said that the scarcity of the above-mentioned resources - coupled with a lack of water - have crippled the local economy.[26]

Construction and Furnishing of a Block of Three Classrooms with VIP Toilets at Community Primary School

Project Location: Ihune Kwagu Akpugo, Akamu West LGA, Enugu East Senatorial District

Cost: N30 million

On September 22, 2017, the Tracka team visited the community of Ihune Kwagu for the first time. At the time of the visit, the school had only one block of four classrooms. Each of the rooms was used as an administrative office. On May 20, 2018, the team revisited the community only to find that nothing had been done to advance the improvement project. Calls placed to Rep. Chukwuemeka Ujam of the Nkanu East/West Federal Constituency were said to have been a dead end.[27]

Construction of Link Bridge Between Malla-Inna and Kargarawal Communities

Project Location: Malla-Inna and Kargarawal Communities

Cost: N15 million

The lack of a workable bridge linking Malla-Inna and Kargarawal has been a matter of deep concern to both communities. The bridge was meant to boost agricultural, economic and educational activities. During Tracka's advocacy meeting with members of the communities, however, they discovered that the construction was not done and the environment had been degraded by erosion, making it difficult for school children to access their learning institutions. It was clear that the communities remain separated and business between them paralyzed.[28]

Renovation of One Block of Classrooms

Project Location: Obile-Ohaji in Ohaji/Egbema/Oguta/Oru West Federal Constituency

Cost: N13 million

Few in this constituency were even aware of this project when the Tracka team visited the area. At the end of a town hall meeting with community heads, they wound up drafting letters to their representative, Goodluck Opia Nanah, requesting an update on the project implementation status.[29]

At the close of 2017, the project was reportedly still undone. In addition, Tracka noted that residents viewed the project as a misplaced priority in that its objectives did not address what they identified as major needs in the community.[30]

Construction and Furnishing of Two Classroom Blocks

Project Location: Chikun LGA, Kaduna State

Cost: N57 million

The location of this project is not clearly stated, but should be somewhere in the Chikun local government area. The Tracka PTO outlines a pathetic situation regarding the only school in Agawan Na Maigaro, where pupils do their lessons under trees. The report also notes that the primary school should have over 600 pupils, but due to a dearth of infrastructure, many of them refuse to attend school. As the project remains unfinished, the number of out-of-school children in the country continues to increase.[31]

Purchase of Grains for Internally Displaced Persons

Project Location: Widil/Garko Federal Constituency

Cost: N10 million

In 2017, a project tracking officer visited the Garko community in order to monitor the execution of a constituency project that was supposed to provide grains to internally displaced people in the area. Some members of Garko Progressive Alliance, however, revealed that there were no displaced persons in their community. Members suggested that the $N10 million nominated for such a project could have been used to solve the problem of water scarcity instead.[32] This shows an utter disconnect between some Nigerian legislators and the constituencies they represent. It also goes to show that their constituents are not part of the budget processes.[33]

Completion of Civic Center, Agasa Obehina Junction, Okene

Project Location: Kogi Central Senatorial District

Cost: N64,333,333 (2016 budget) and N40 million (2017 budget)

Some projects appear to be white elephants in nature. These projects seem so big that, year in and year out, they stay there just to gulp millions of naira. This is the situation with the civic center project. It first appeared in the 2016 budget and was recaptured in 2017, but the project remained unfinished, with little progress year after year.[34]

Erosion and Flood Control In Kichita

Project Location: Kwara North Senatorial District

Cost: N52 million (2016 budget) and N60 million (2017 budget)

Kichita, a vibrant, agrarian area in Kwara State, is located on a flood plain, making it ideal for agriculture. The area, however, is at risk of flooding whenever it rains heavily, which has necessitated effective flood control measures. The Kichita road project was nominated by Sen. Mohammed Shaa'ba Lafiagi, representing Kwara North Senatorial District in 2016, and was again nominated for appropriation in 2017. Despite these repeated nominations, the project has been abandoned on several occasions, leaving the community at risk with each flood.[35]

Training of Youths On Renewable Energy

Project Location: Agege Federal Constituency

Cost: N40 million

Despite the reported release of 70% of the money allocated for this project, the Tracka team labeled it unfinished. The proposed training, which was designed to teach youths how to construct solar panels, was aimed at developing entrepreneurial skills among young people. A visit by the Tracka team to the Agege Federal Constituency, however, revealed that no preparation for implementation was in place. Attempts at contacting Aderanijo Taofeek Abiodun, their representative in the Green Chamber, proved unsuccessful.[36]

Renovation of Schools (Dikko Primary School, Boroji Primary School, Etsu Tasha Primary School, Kagba Primary School)

Project Location: Edati LGA, Mokwa Federal Constituency

Cost: N8 million

The last renovation that reportedly took place in this area was in 1989/90. Despite the call for these projects, however, It was discovered that no attempt had been made to implement any of them. With the help of the Tracka PTO, the community wrote a letter to Ahmed Abu, their federal representative, requesting an update on the project. At the time of this report, there has been no response.[37]

Youth Development Center

Project Location: Jega Community, Kebbi State

Cost: N41 million

This is a non-existent youth center constituency project from the 2017 budget that was facilitated by Mr. Muhammad Umar Jega. According to Tracka, Jega represented the Gwandu/Aliero/Jega federal constituency of Kebbi State in the national assembly at the time. The project has become a subject of controversy, since a visit by the Tracka team in April of 2018 revealed that there was nothing where the youth center project was slated to exist.

Mr. Emmanuel Yaro, a Tracka official in Kebbi state, said there was no such project in Jega as claimed by the lawmaker. When Tracka sought Muhammad Jega's explanation, the lawmaker refused to respond.[39]

YEAR 2018

Construction Of Classroom Block, Office And Toilet

Project Location: Ogwulube Ebenebe Community, Awka North LGA, Anambra Central Senatorial District, Anambra State.

Cost: N15 million

According to another Tracka report, members of Ogwulube Ebenebe community in Anambra State were in disbelief when they heard of the N15 million classroom project at Eze Eke Primary School Umuohi-Okija. It was the first time they had heard of such a project. The project was supposed to be a concrete way of boosting children's education in Ogwulube Ebenebe but it was abandoned as of November 2019, thus denying children better access to education. Even when funds were disbursed, only a skeletal building was constructed and that was later abandoned, according to Tracka.[40]

Rural Electrification Project

Project Location: Kale To Biro To Olooyo In Surulere LGA, Oyo State

Cost: N37 million

During the Tracka team's visits to Kale, Biro, and Olooyo communities in Surulere Local Government Area of Oyo State in September 2018, they made community leaders and residents aware of an interesting project that had approximately two consecutive years of work already scheduled, though no meaningful work had been carried out. Despite the huge amount of money that had been allocated, the project was only completed in Olooyo, while the communities of Kale and Biro were left with no electricity. A visit to the communities in October of 2019 revealed that the transformer supplied to Biro was not connected to any power source. Only electric poles were erected in Kale, leaving the communities in darkness.[41]

Empowerment/Skill Acquisition for Youths and Women

Project Location: Ikono/ Ini Federal Constituency, Akwa Ibom

Cost: N50 million

The empowerment and skill acquisition program for youths and women in these Akwa Ibom communities was captured in the budget, nominated by Rep. Iboro Ekanem. But as Tracka engaged the community, it was evident that they were not aware of any empowerment program, nor any project whatsoever in the are[42]. A visit to the communities by the

Tracka team revealed that no such project had been executed as of the first half of 2019.[43]

Provision of Pupils' Desks and Chairs to Schools

Project Location: Ogbolomabiri, Okoroma Clan, Nembe in Nembe LGA, Bayelsa State.

Cost: N50 million

In search of the above project, Tracka visited the communities from Ogbolomabiri to Okoroma to Opu-Nembe, discovering that this project did not have traceable proposed sites in any of the communities.[44]

Supply and Installation of 500 KVA Transformer

Project Location: Orile-Oko in Remo North LGA, Ogun East Senatorial District, Ogun State

Cost: N9 million

Out of the five transformer projects nominated as constituency projects by Sen. Buruji Kashamu in 2018, only the one at Orile Oko was reportedly completed, with others abandoned as of November 2019.[45]

Provision of Six Motorized Boreholes with Generator

Project Location: Idah, Igalamela-Odolu, Ofu and Ibaji Federal Constituency Kogi State

Cost: N30 million

In the 2017 budget, six motorized boreholes with power generators were nominated for the Idah/Igalamela-Odolu/Ofu and Ibaji communities. After many months of monitoring, Tracka discovered that only one borehole was installed in the community, though $N30 million was allocated for the project.[46] In the 2018 budget, the same project title was captured at $N30 million. In June 2019, Tracka again visited the beneficiary communities to assess progress, but the team discovered that nothing had been done.[47]

Amaeke Ishiagu Erosion Control Road Project

Project Location: Ivo LGA, Ebonyi State

Cost: N30 million

N30 million was allocated in 2018 for the Amaeke Ishiagu Erosion Control Road Project, in Ivo LGA of Ebonyi State. According to Tracka in a February 2021 tweet, the project has been abandoned.[48]

YEAR 2019

Construction of Sport Ground

Project Location: Ahiaba Secondary School, Obingwa Local Government Area of Abia State

Cost: N30 million

Mr. Enyinnaya Abaribe, a senator from Abia State, facilitated the construction of a sport ground in Ahiaba Secondary School in Obingwa LGA of Abia State in 2019 at the cost of N30 million. The constituency project remains abandoned two years after funds were released by the federal government.[49]

Construction of a Mini-Stadium

Project Location: Osisioma Ngwa LGA, Osisioma/Ugwunagbo/Obingwa Federal Constituency, Abia State

Cost: N60 million (in 2019 budget) and N60 million (in 2020 budget)

N60 million each was allocated in the 2019 and 2020 FG ZIPs, respectively, for the construction of a mini-stadium in Osisioma Ngwa LGA, Osisioma/Ugwunagbo/Obingwa Federal Constituency, Abia State. In January 2021, Tracka reported via tweet that despite 50% of funds having been released, the project remains abandoned. [50]

Construction of 4 Classroom Block, Office and Toilet

Project Location: Aguluzigbo in Anaocha LGA, Anambra Central Senatorial District, Anambra State

Cost: N20 million

N20 million was allocated in the 2019 FG ZIP for the construction of a four-classroom block with office and toilet at Community High School, Aguluzigbo in Anaocha LGA, Anambra Central Senatorial District, Anambra State. This came at the recommendation of Senator Victor Umeh, representing the district at the Red Chambers. Tracka's report states that the project has been abandoned.[51]

Construction of 4-Classroom Block, Office and Toilet

Project Location: Etiti Idemili Awka South LGA, Anambra Central Senatorial District, Anambra State

Cost: N15 million

N15 million was allocated in the 2019 FG ZIP for the construction of a four-classroom block with office and toilet at Girls Secondary School, Etiti Idemili Awka South LGA, Anambra Central Senatorial District, Anambra State. The project, nominated by Sen. Uche Ekwunife and awarded to Biyaks Business Options Ltd, is reportedly abandoned.[52]

Construction of 4-Classroom Block With Office And Toilet

Project Location: Igwedimma Primary School, Awka South LGA, Anambra Central Senatorial District, Anambra State

Cost: N15 million

Sen. Uche Ekwunife nominated this project as well, which has N15 million allocated to it. This project, which is the construction of a four-classroom block with office and toilet at Igwedimma Primary School, Awka South LGA, Anambra Central Senatorial District, has been abandoned, according to Tracka's January 13, 2021 tweet. The project was awarded to Del-Bito Construction Services Ltd.[53]

Construction of Solar-Powered Borehole with Overhead Tank

Project Location: Eziowelle, Idemili North LGA, Anambra Central Senatorial District, Anambra State

Cost: N15 million

N15 million was allocated in the 2019 budget for the construction of a solar powered borehole with an overhead tank at Eke Market Square, Eziowelle in Idemili North LGA, Anambra Central Senatorial District, Anambra State. The project, facilitated by Sen. Victor Umeh, is reportedly abandoned.[54]

Construction of Type 1 Primary Healthcare Centre

Project Location: Lainde, Girei LGA, Adamawa State

Cost: N25 million

In January of 2021, Tracka tweeted that the construction of a primary healthcare centre at Lainde, Girei LGA in Adamawa State was poorly implemented, despite massive amounts of money budgeted for the project. The construction of the health facility cost $N25 million and was allocated in the 2019 FG ZIP which contained provisions for landscaping, parking lots, and fencing.[55]

YEAR 2020

Supply of Motorcycles to Youths

Project Location: Funtua/Dandume Federal Constituency, Katsina State

Cost: N25 million

N25 million was allocated in the 2020 FG ZIP for the supply of motorcycles to youths in Funtua/Dandume Federal Constituency in Katsina State. Tracka reported that 30 motorcycles were supplied and given to selected beneficiaries, including police and National Drug Law Enforcement Agency personnel, though they were labeled as donations.[56]

Construction of Three Classroom Blocks, Office and Toilet

Project Location: Razat, Barkin Ladi LGA, Plateau State

Cost: N30 million

N30 million was allocated to the construction of three classroom blocks, office accommodations, and toilets in Razat,

Barkin Ladi LGA of Plateau State. According to Tracka, the project was left abandoned by the contractor as of February 2021.[57]

Design and Construction of 2 Blocks Of 40 K- Clamp Open Stalls

Mmahu Market in Egbema, Ohaji Egbema LGA, Imo West Senatorial District
Imo state

Cost: N8.8 million

$N8,870,000 was allocated in the 2020 ZIP for the design and construction of open stalls at Mmahu Market, Egbema Ohaji/Egbema LGA, Imo West Senatorial District, Imo State. Tracka reported that the project has been abandoned by the contractor as of February 2021.[58]

Strategic Empowerment for Women

Project Location: Okitipupa/Irele Federal Constituency, Ondo State

Cost: N23.7 million

In 2020, $N23,750,000 was allocated to what was described as the Strategic Empowerment for Women in Okitipupa/Irele Federal Constituency, Ondo State. Tracka discovered and reported on Twitter that about 100 beneficiaries across the wards were selected, trained, and received $N20,000 as start-up capital.[59] This meager amount of money distributed to beneficiaries is a pale comparison of the over $N23.7 million allotted for this project.

Rural Road Completion Project

Project Location: Agugwu, Umudu Ugwuoba, Oji River LGA, Enugu State

Cost: N60 million

Tracka reported via Twitter that this $N60 million project allocated for the completion of a rural road in Agugwu, Umudu Ugwuoba, Oji River LGA of Enugu State has been abandoned as of February 2021. The organization drew the attention of Sen. Ike Ekweremadu, urging him to reach out to the contractor.[60]

Construction of Community Town Hall

Project Location: Tabat in Langtang North LGA, Plateau State

Cost: N20 million

$N20 million was allocated in the 2020 FG ZIP for the construction of a community town hall at Tabat in Langtang North LGA, Plateau State. Tracka reveals, however, that the project has been abandoned and the property converted to a church.[61]

CHAPTER FIVE

Exiting The Evil Cycle

If Nigeria continues with this chain of abandonments, it will continue to sustain a monumental waste of resources. The perpetual waste will leave available funds too meager to finance newly initiated projects. The cost of both materials and labor tend to increase over time, and when lean funds cannot finance the projects, this leads to abandonment, causing a vicious cycle where the resources are then wasted again. This is an evil cycle that continues to keep Nigeria miserably and permanently fixed in a trap of crumbling or non-existent infrastructure and stunted human development. There is no way Nigeria could look like a developed country or appear rich in commensuration with its vast natural wealth if its project management approach stays entrapped in an evil cycle of abandonments.

As years go by, the number of abandoned projects continues to reinforce the evil cycle that cages Nigeria's prosperity. In 2011, for instance, a report from the Presidential Projects Assessment Committee headed by Ibrahim Bunu puts the number of abandoned federal projects at 11,886. This represents an estimated $N7.78 trillion in waste.[1] By 2017, only six years later, the number of abandoned projects in the country soared to about 56,000 - representing a total cost of $N12 trillion - according to a survey by the Chartered Institute of Project Managers of Nigeria.[2] If Nigeria stays on this trajectory for the next dozen years, the total number of abandoned projects could easily skyrocket to 100,000.

Let's assume that in the next ten years, an administration comes to power determined to complete the 100,000+ projects initiated and abandoned in past years. Such an administration might have the best of intentions, but would not have the capacity to embark on new projects and could also face difficulty in completing such a vast number of abandoned projects within its tenure of only four or eight years. The cycle is fixed, and the cycle is evil. This appears to be one fundamental reason why Nigeria does not prosper, and may not become a developed country for decades. This evil cycle will continue to systematically undercut the economic potential of the country, reducing economic opportunities and draining its citizens. Some citizens, in fact, prefer to move to foreign countries in search of better - or indeed, any - opportunities at all.

It appears that any administration wishing to catapult Nigeria into first-world status in terms of infrastructural and socio-economic development must first devise a plan to exit the evil cycle continued by years of abandoning projects and wasting resources. Without exiting this cyclical sequence, all efforts geared toward development will not likely yield good results. As far as the evil cycle is concerned, the Nigerian government will continue to fail its citizens because the system is conditioned to doom every attempt at progress and prosperity. It only births another shade of evil when the country is driven to primordial acquisition of loans to fund budgets for capital projects, which later live on as taxes for future generations. In fact, The Guardian reported in February of 2021 that the federal government disregarded the Central Bank of Nigeria Act (2007) as it moved to restructure its estimated $25.6 billion in overdrafts into a 30 year debt.[3] This means the converted debt, worth almost $N10 trillion, would be amortized over 30 years, subjecting Nigerians to agonizing taxation for decades to come. Do not forget that it was the lean resources that necessitated the need for excessive borrowing in the first place. In justifying Nigeria's rising debt, Director-General of the Debt Management Office (DMO)

Patience Oniha was once quoted as saying that loans were needed to improve infrastructure and to create jobs in Nigeria, where unemployment has been projected to rise to 33.5% by 2021, according to the Nigeria Employers' Consultative Association (NECA).[4] That may be true, but what happens when these accumulated loans are expended on projects that turn out to be abandoned? It means that Nigerians waste more money, and on projects that fail to meet the purposes for which they were intended. Despite numerous loans acquired by Buhari's government to invest in projects meant to boost wealth creation and stimulate growth, the Nigerian Bureau of Statistics reported Nigeria's unemployment rate to have risen from 27.1% in the second quarter of 2020 to 33.3% in the fourth quarter of 2020. This indicates that the loans are consumed by the influences of the evil cycle.

If Nigerian leaders continue to seek self-glorification through projects they initiate and conclude, and if they take other leaders' projects as competition best dealt with by abandonment, then the majority of projects will continue to fail. In other words, incumbents who continue to see their predecessors' projects as mementos of past leadership will continue to let them lay fallow, since in their view, they only stand to compete against their own achievements. For this reason, they will continue to find ways to outshine the past by undermining the efforts of their predecessors. This harmful clawing for individualistic legacy absolutely buries the spirit of collectivist ownership and continuity of government projects.

It is clear that the transition of power from one political party to another stands as a major cause of project abandonment in Nigeria. This will not soon cease, since partisan rivalries thrive on popularity, and they operate under the notion that by disparaging the ideas and initiatives of a rival political party, it can kill its popularity. A political party will come to power and mock the legacy projects of the former ruling party, seeking to dismantle them, and setting new paradigms to show superiority. Most parties use their power to punish constituencies where they did not get many votes by ignoring ongoing projects in their domain. This is one of the factors that kill many Nigerian projects. Corruption is just another fundamental problem bedeviling project implementation in Nigeria as many leaders contrive projects and programs and render them conduits through which public funds are looted.

Besides the foregoing, causal factors of initiative abandonment are abundant in Nigeria. They include but are not limited to: corruption, poor project monitoring, contract splitting, death of contractors, increase in prices of materials, community unrest, etc. The overall effect, however, is primarily the wastage of resources. It is this waste of resources that depletes the country's treasury and makes it incapable of meeting the fundamental needs of the citizenry. If the trends of abandonment and wastage are not reversed, Nigeria could find itself amongst the least fancied nations and worst places on earth for visits and business partnerships.

So how can Nigeria exit this perennial evil cycle? It is very simple. The method is not a strange one, nor is it a novel strategy to the country itself. The basic answer to this nagging question of discontinuity of government initiatives is simply for the country to formulate a long-term national plan that will revolutionize infrastructural setup. This is bound to fail as well, however, unless it is managed more efficiently than anything the country has seen up to this point.

Before we proceed further, let us ask a question: how did countries like Qatar, United Arab Emirates, and Singapore become popular destinations and centers of world-wide admiration as they compete against the Western world with their state-of-the-art infrastructures and high standards of living? In each case, a long-term national planning approach did the trick. They handled major, progressive projects in such a way that prioritized continuity, letting them flow easily through the odds and vagaries of power politics.

When Qatar National Vision 2030 (QNV2030) first launched in October of 2008 by the General Secretariat for Development Planning, Qatar set a roadmap in place that would help transform the country into an advanced society capable of sustainable development with the ultimate aim of providing a higher standard of living to the citizenry by 2030. This laudable national plan was initiated under the leadership of Emir Hamad bin Khalifa, who handed it over in 2013 to his son, Sheikh Tamim bin Hamad al-Thani. Since then, the successor has continued with the pursuit of this master vision. Apart from assisting the Qatari government in policy-making, including planning and allocation of funds toward specified targets, this long-term vision also provides the private sector with collective direction. Indeed, many companies are reportedly making references to QNV2030 in their mission statements.[5] While this small Islamic country is rapidly developing in tourism, real estate, transportation, and other key infrastructures under QNV2030, the year 2022 was set as a mid-term deadline for the delivery of top projects for the hosting of 2022 FIFA World Cup.

With the Qatari government budgeting over $200 billion as part of a major infrastructure investment scheme, the construction sector is booming in Qatar.[6] This sector is creating a lot of employment, as well as attracting investors. The country is already reaping the fruit of QNV2030. According to USA Today in 2019, Qatar's population of 2.6 million is by far the richest country in the world with a GNI per capita of $116,799, more than $20,000 higher than any other nation.[7] The country also has the lowest unemployment rate in the world at 0.2%.[8] This is a result of diligent long-term planning.

Another small nation that breaks free from the underdeveloped league of third world countries is the United Arab Emirates (UAE) and it, too, has been a result of careful planning. This country strategically plans its economy around its most populous city, Dubai.[9] Since the 1970s, the UAE government has invested heavily in the construction of infrastructure, which it regards as the basis for economic and social development, and great focus is also placed on aviation and tourism. This combination creates a favorable environment for foreign capital to fly into Dubai.[10]

UAE came up with Vision 2021 during a cabinet meeting in 2010 headed by Vice President and Prime Minister Sheikh Mohammed bin Rashid Al Maktoum. The vision was guided by the National Work Program, launched by President Sheikh Khalifa Bin Zayed Al Nahyan, then adopted by other rulers of the Emirates and members of the Federal Supreme Council.[11] This vision was formulated to place the UAE among the most developed countries in the world by 2021, its Golden Jubilee marking 50 years from the formation of the UAE on December 2, 1971. Next is a 50-year strategy for national development known as the UAE Centennial 2071 Vision, which is aimed at enabling its citizens to live in the best country in the world.[12]

The UAE plans have helped target a sustainable environment, create infrastructure, and grow a scientifically-based economy driven by research and innovation. Today, Nigerian politicians are traveling to Dubai in droves for vacation and shopping. The city has become one of the most desirable destinations in the world due to its massive infrastructural upgrade and high-tech economy.

Singapore must not be overlooked when it comes to using strategic long-term plans to transform an under-developed society into a world-class destination and hub of international economy. Singapore was a backwater of development when British colonialists left in 1963, and even when it separated from Malaysia to become independent in 1965, the country was in a very poor state. When asked about the transformation, renowned master planner Dr. Liu Thai Ker mentioned short-term and long-term plans that were put in place to effect the total evolution of Singapore from a tiny, backward country to a well-developed city-state.

According to Liu Thai Ker, "When the British left, Singapore was actually a very backward country. Just to describe what it was like, in 1960, we had approximately 1.6 million people, of which nearly three out of four lived in squatter colonies or slums.[13]... As early as 1965, we embarked on the Koenigsberger ring-shaped plan, which was completed in 1967. After that, we decided to prepare the Concept Plan 1971 with the help of United Nations Development Programme (UNDP). These 1967 and 1971 plans gave... a good starting point to plan the 1991 Concept Plan, with the objective of upgrading Singapore further to a World Class city."[14]

It is not that Nigeria has not formulated policies geared toward development like Qatar, UAE, and Singapore. In fact on several occasions, Nigeria has developed long-term plans for infrastructural and socio-economic development. Some of them are well-conceived and articulated, but lack clear direction. Some plans lack cross-party consultation, public commitment, continuity, popularity, and discipline. Umaru Yar'Adua's Vision 2020 is one example. It was well-conceptualized with priorities of developing an integrated intermodal transport system as well as putting an adequate power supply and technology-centered education in place to ensure Nigeria's capability of developing into an industrialized nation by the year 2020. As noted elsewhere, the vision died with the demise of President Yar'Adua.

Vision 2050, a successor plan to Vision 20:2020 that was inaugurated by President Muhammadu Buhari in September 2020, may also fail in directing government agencies to follow a definite and continuous pathway toward implementation of projects, programs, and policies. The reason has to do with lack of wide consultation with critical stakeholders, as well as failure to collect input from the Nigerian public. Such moves could have earned the vision wider acceptability. The country might continue to waste resources through abandonment of initiatives if Vision 2050's blueprint fails to introduce critical projects, programs, and policies for government administration, and also to guide successive leaders in leaving the country with the best possible infrastructure. This could place Nigeria among the top 20 economies in the world by the year 2050.

Lack of cohesion and unity of purpose among Nigerian political leaders is drawing the country backward. It causes the country to be all moves but no movement, never quite clearing the hurdle toward concrete development. In this environment, the fundamental challenge of Vision 2050 is that if Buhari leaves office, and a political party other than APC takes over, there is a high probability that the Vision will fail or be discarded in favor of another buzzword.

Vision 2050 could offer the country an opportunity to end the regime of disjointed priorities that facilitate abandonment of projects, programs, and policies. Before it becomes too late, Nigerian government should call for nationwide town hall meetings and engage executives of all political parties as a matter of urgent importance. Legislators, ex-presidents, civil engineers, public project contractors, civil society organizations, academia, captains of industries, financial institutions, traditional rulers, estate valuers, youth leaders, executives of organized labor groups, service chiefs, women leaders, religious leaders, media, and other relevant stakeholders should be brought together in an ongoing effort to work toward a common goal. The input of these stakeholders should form a concise blueprint that can successfully capture all the essentials that Nigeria needs over the next 30 years. This would convey a sense of collective ownership of projects, programs, and policies. To ensure that implementation is not sabotaged by change of government, the policy blueprint should pass through legislation, then be held accountable by a pre-determined semi-annual budget. Since legislative function has to do with checks and balances, the National Assembly should ensure that executives do not introduce unvetted projects into the budget. Programs and policies that hamper the grand vision should be strictly prohibited.

There should be a specialized court in Nigeria to handle cases of corruption. This would help to avoid delays in addressing cases of misappropriation of public funds. This court should have jurisdiction in trying past leaders, contractors, and others related to public project abandonments.

The sooner Nigeria realizes that it is in an evil cycle of project abandonment, the better chance they have to find a way out of it. Policies on accountability must be reviewed and strengthened. A look at the management of zonal intervention projects or constituency projects nominated by the legislators reveals clear cases of opacity, irregularities, and daylight robbery, and all of those need to be stopped. There should be a checklist for annual constituency projects made available to all local government councils, and information should be sent to the community leadership of the areas where the projects are designated. This would provide transparency and accountability, enabling people to follow the trajectory of the projects in their area, and giving them the ability to solve problems and make adjustments as needed.

These steps, if taken, could result in the completion of nearly every project that is initiated. Since constituency projects were primarily conceived to bring development closer to the people, government officials should be involved in the entire process since they are the spokespeople for the citizens. This approach would help bring out initiatives that are essential to the communities, leaving behind those that are dispensable and do not serve the citizens at all.

Endnotes

CHAPTER ONE

[1] SFUHEATHROWCASE.WORDPRESS.COM. "Heathrow Terminal 5 Case Study" https://sfuheathrowcase.wordpress.com

[2] Ibid.

[3] Effiong, Aloy (2012). Government And Political Development In Nigeria. Uyo: MEF (Nigeria) Ltd, p.3.

[4] Ibid. p.21

[5] OPEN.LIB.UMN.EDU. "Sociology." https://open.lib.umn.edu/sociology/chapter/14-1-power-and-authority/

[6] Ibid.

[7] Institute On Governance (March 2011) The Governance in Continuum: Origins & Conceptual Construct, p.16.

[8] Ayobami, Abimbola (November 24, 2012) "About 12,000 Federal Projects Abandoned Across Nigeria" https://www.premiumtimesng.com/news/108450-about-12000-federal-projects-abandoned-across-nigeria.html

[9] Ibid.

CHAPTER TWO

[1] Greene, Robert (1998). The 48 Laws of Power. London: Profile Books Ltd, 1998, P.347.

[2] Ibid., p.349.

[3] Ibid.

[4] Ibid.

[5] Sobowale. (19 January 2015). "Return of abandoned projects" https://www.vanguardngr.com/2015/01/return-abandoned-projects/

[6] Feyisipo, Remi (September 2020). "Makinde Will Not Abandon Projects Like His Immediate Predecessor – Olatubosun." https://businessday.ng/politics/article/makinde-will-not-abandon-projects-like-his-immediate-predecessor-olatubosun/

[7] Adebowale, Segun (20 December 2014) "Alao-Akala to Ajimobi: Stop Projecting My Achievements As Yours" Theeagleonline.com. https://theeagleonline.com.ng/alao-akala-to-ajimobi-stop-projecting-my-achievements-as-yours/

[8] Centre for Democracy and Development (July 2018). Ekiti State 2018 Governorship Election, p.14

⁹ Obichie, Buchi (7 November 2018). "I won't abandon Fayose's projects – Fayemi." https://www.legit.ng/1202725-i-wont-abandon-fayoses-projects

¹⁰ Balogun, Wole (5 July 2018) "Ekiti Abandoned Projects Begging For Attention" The Sun Nigeria. https://www.sunnewsonline.com/ekiti-abandoned-projects-begging-attention/

¹¹ Oluwole, Josiah (5 November 2018). "Fayemi, Fayose Bicker Over Abandonment Of Projects In Ekiti" Premiumtimesng.com. https://www.premiumtimesng.com/regional/ssouth-west/294262-fayemi-fayose-bicker-over-abandonment-of-projects-in-ekiti.html

¹² Ibid.

¹³ Ibid.

¹⁴ Ibid.

¹⁵ Ogugbuaja, Charles (25 December 2020). "Stop demolishing my legacy projects, Okorocha tells Uzodimma" The Guardian. https://guardian.ng/politics/stop-demolishing-my-legacy-projects-okorocha-tells-uzodimma/

¹⁶ Ibid.

¹⁷ Ibid.

[18] Ibid.

[19] Urhobotoday.com. "Okowa Slams Uduaghan Over Abandoned Trans-Warri/Ode-Itsekiri Road Project" https://urhobotoday.com/?p=31898

[20] Ibid.

[21] Fasan, Olu (7 January 2021). "Kukah's Vilification: Buhari is Fighting the Wrong 'Enemy'" in: Vanguard, p.16.

[22] Senator John James Akpanudoedeghe's speech on November 9, 2020 during his visit to Akwa Ibom State Council of Nigerian Union of Journalists (NUJ) in Uyo, Akwa Ibom State.

[23] Thenationonlineng.net (22 October 2017). "Abandoned Rivers State Monorail Project" https://thenationonlineng.net/abandoned-rivers-state-monorail-project/

[24] Chukwu, Ignatius & Gladys Nweke (2 February 2019). "Rivers N150bn Monorail Project Tears Candidates Apart" Businessday.ng. https://businessday.ng/politics/article/rivers-n150bn-monorail-project-tears-candidates-apart/

[25] Akasike, Chukwudi (29 March 2016). "Rivers Abandons Monorail Project" Punchng.com. https://punchng.com/rivers-abandons-monorail-project/

²⁶ Ibid.

²⁷ Nwadike, Ogubundu (2 February 2021). "Uzodinma's Administration: One (1) Year of Colossal Failure" being a Press Statement Issued by the Imo State Chapter of the Peoples' Democratic Party (PDP).

²⁸ Ibid.

²⁹ Ibid.

³⁰ Ibid.

³¹ Ibid.

³² Ibid.

³³ Ibid.

³⁴ Ibid.

³⁵ Ibid.

³⁶ Ibid.

³⁷ Jumbo-Asukwo, Ferdinand (12 August 2018). "Ex-CP Atiku Abubakar Lambasts President Buhari Over N-Power, Restructuring" Today.ng. https://www.today.ng/news/politics/atiku-abubakar-lambasts-president-buhari-power-restructuring-141199

³⁸ Sunday, Marygift (21 July 2020). "News NDDC Spent N4.2b In One Day, Akpabio Tells Reps" Fresh1059fm.com.

https://fresh1059fm.com/nddc-spent-n4-2b-in-one-day-akpabio-tells-reps/

[39] Dailytrust.com (26 July 2020) "Uncompleted NDDC projects dot Niger Delta"https://dailytrust.com/uncompleted-nddc-projects-dot-niger-delta

[40] Jannah, Chijioke (28 October 2019) "Why NDDC abandoned 12,000 projects in Niger-Delta – Akpabio" Dailypost.ng. https://dailypost.ng/2019/10/28/why-nddc-abandoned-12000-projects-in-niger-delta-akpabio/

CHAPTER THREE

[1] BudgIT (2019). Investing In People: Discussion Notes. Lagos, p.11.

[2] Ibid.

[3] Ibid.

[4] Ibid.

[5] Ibid.

[6] Ibid.

[7] Agbese, Dan (1 June 2018). "The missing $16 billion and the Missing Power" Guardian.ng > https://guardian.ng/opinion/the-missing-16-billion-and-the-missing-power/

[8] Ibid.

[9] Ibid.

[10] Ibid.

[11] Nextedition.com.ng (17 February 2021). "FG Spends Over N50bn Monthly On Electricity – Minister" https://www.nextedition.com.ng/fg-spends-over-n50bn-monthly-on-electricity-minister

[12] Ibid.

[13] Reuters (20 February 2018). "Nigerian State Oil Firm Spent $5.8 Bln On Fuel Imports Since Late 2017" https://www.reuters.com/article/nigeria-oil-idUSL8N1QA6LR

[14] Nnpcgroup.com. "Greenfield Refinery Initiative" https://nnpcgroup.com/NNPC-Business/Midstream-Ventures/Pages/Greenfield-Refinery-Initiative.aspx

[15] Ibid.

[16] Africaoilgasreport.com (9 November 2018). "Probe the failure of Government's Greenfield Crude Oil Refineries in Nigeria" africaoilgasreport.com> https://africaoilgasreport.com/2018/11/refining-gap/probe-the-failure-of-governments-greenfield-crude-oil-refineries-in-nigeria/

[17] Ayobami, Abimbola (24 November 2012) "About 12,000 Federal Projects Abandoned Across Nigeria" premiumtimesng.com > https://www.premiumtimesng.com/news/108450-about-12000-federal-projects-abandoned-across-nigeria.html

[18] Ibid.

[19] Ibid.

[20] Proshareng.com (21 July 2020). "Mining: Resuscitation of Ajaokuta Steel Company – An End In Sight?" https://www.proshareng.com/news/Oil%20&%20Gas/Mining

--Resuscitation-of-Ajaokuta-Steel-Company---An-End-in-Sight--/52422

[21] Ibid.

[22] Ayobami, Abimbola (24 November 2012) "About 12,000 Federal Projects Abandoned Across Nigeria" Premiumtimesng.com> /https://www.premiumtimesng.com/news/108450-about-12000-federal-projects-abandoned-across-nigeria.html

[23] Udonquak, Aniefiok (5 January 2020). "What is new about Ibom Blue Sea Science and Technology project?" Businessday.ng > https://businessday.ng/features/article/what-is-new-about-ibom-blue-sea-science-and-technology-project/

[24] Akpan-Nsoh, Inemesit (27 December 2018) "Akpabio sabotaged Takeoff Of Ibom Science Park, Group" Guardian.ng > https://m.guardian.ng/news/akpabio-sabotaged-takeoff-of-ibom-science-park-group-alleges/

[25] Udonquak, Aniefiok (5 January 2020). "What is new about Ibom Blue Sea Science and Technology project?" Businessday.ng > https://businessday.ng/features/article/what-is-new-about-ibom-blue-sea-science-and-technology-project/

[26] Yusuf, Kabir (20 August 2020). "Despite High Earnings, Imo, Akwa Ibom, Rivers, Record Highest Unemployment Rates" Premiumtimesng.com > https://www.premiumtimesng.com/news/top-news/409803-de

spite-high-earnings-imo-akwa-ibom-rivers-record-high-unemployment-rates.html

[27] Ochayi, Chris (26 August 2020). "FG will Deliver 337km East-West Road by December 2021 – Akpabio" Vanguardngr.com> https://www.vanguardngr.com/2020/08/fg-will-deliver-337km-east-west-road-by-december-2021-akpabio/

[28] Ibid.

[29] Ogune, Matthew (13 November 2020). "East West Road To Cost N1 Trillion At Completion, Says Akpabio" Guardian.ng > https://guardian.ng/news/east-west-road-to-cost-n1-trillion-at-completion-says-akpabio/

[30] Bassey, Okon (14 December 2020) "Champion Breweries Appeals to FG to Fix Calabar -Itu Road" Thisdaylive.com> https://www.thisdaylive.com/index.php/2020/12/14/champion-breweries-appeals-to-fg-to-fix-calabar-itu-road/

[31] Ibid.

[32] Ibid.

[33] BudgiT (2019). Investing In People: Discussion Notes. Lagos, p.13

[34] Busari, Kemi (27 January 2018). "INVESTIGATION: At Nigeria's Abandoned Nuclear Centre, Failed Projects, Idle Staff And 'Fraud' [Part 2]" Premiumtimesng.com>

[35] Ibid.

[36] Ibid.

[37] Ibid.

[38] Ibid.

[39] Ibid.

[40] Onyeji, Ebuka (19 January 2020). "Analysis: Why Nigeria's Vision 20:2020 Was Bound To Fail" Premiumtimesng.com> https://www.premiumtimesng.com/news/top-news/373321-analysis-why-nigerias-vision-202020-was-bound-to-fail.html

[41] Ola, Rasheedat Ola (23 January 2009). "Yar'Adua's Seven Point Agenda: any hope for the Nigerian people?" Marxist.com> https://www.marxist.com/yaraduas-seven-point-agenda-nigeria.htm

[42] Onyeji, Ebuka (19 January 2020). "Analysis: Why Nigeria's Vision 20:2020 Was Bound To Fail" https://www.premiumtimesng.com/news/top-news/373321-analysis-why-nigerias-vision-202020-was-bound-to-fail.html

[43] Oladipo, Dotun (1 April 2012). "Vision 2020: Autopsy of Policy Failure" Theeagleonline.com.ng> https://theeagleonline.com.ng/vision-2020-autopsy-of-policy-failure/

[44] Ibid.

[45] Adetayo, Olalekan (10 September 2020). "Buhari Inaugurates Committee for Vision 2050" Punchng.com> htttps://punchng.com/buhari-inaugurates-committee-for-vision-2050/

[46] Onyeji, Ebuka (19 January 2020). "Analysis: Why Nigeria's Vision 20:2020 Was Bound To Fail" https://www.premiumtimesng.com/news/top-news/373321-analysis-why-nigerias-vision-202020-was-bound-to-fail.html

[47] Onyeji, Ebuka (19 January 2020). https://www.premiumtimesng.com/news/top-news/373321-analysis-why-nigerias-vision-202020-was-bound-to-fail.html

CHAPTER FOUR

[1] Van Zyl, Albert. "What Is Wrong With The Constituency Development Funds?" In: International Budget Partnership (IBP) Budget Brief No. 10, available at http://international-budget.org/publications/brief10/

[2] Udefuna Patrick, Fadila Jumare & Francis Ojo Adebayo (July 2013). "Legislative Constituency Project in Nigeria: Implication for National Development" in: Mediterranean Journal of Social Sciences. Rome: MCSER-CEMAS-Sapienza University of Rome, p.647.

[3] Ibid., p. 648.

[4] Daily Trust, Monday August 16, 2010.

[5] Daka, Terhemba & Matthew Ogune (20 November 2019). "N1tr Wasted On Constituency Projects, Says Buhari" Guardian.ng> https://m.guardian.ng/news/n1tr-wasted-on-constituency-projects-says-buhari/

[6] Iredia, Tonnie (24 April 2016) "What Exactly Is The Meaning of Constituency Project?" Vanguardngr.com>https://www.vanguardngr.com/2016/04/exactly-meaning-constituency-project/

[7] Ibid.

[8] Ibid.

[9] Gbajabiamila, Femi (8 March 2013) "Constituency Projects,

Budget Process and Related Matters – Role of Legislature and General Misconceptions" Premiumtimesng.com> www.premiumtimesng.com/opinion/123687-constituency-projects-budget-process-abd-related-matters-role-oflegislature-and-general-misconceptions-by-femi-gbajabiamila.html

[10] BudgIT Tracka (June 2018) 2017 Federal Constituency Projects: Lessons And Findings From Focus States, pp.3& 5

[11] Ibid., p.165.

[12] Ibid., p.166.

[13] Ibid.

[14] Ibid., p.165.

[15] Ibid.

[16] Globalfinancialdigest.com (8 March 2021). "Civil Society Group, Tracka Raises Concerns Over N59 Bln Budget For 'Invisible' Empowerment Projects"> https://globalfinancialdigest.com/civil-society-group-tracka-raises-concerns-over-n59-bln-budget-for-invisible-empowerment-projects/

[17] Ibid.

[18] BudgIT Tracka (June 2018) 2017 Federal Constituency Projects: Lessons And Findings From Focus States, p.165.

[19] Ibid.

[20] Ibid., p.13.

[21] Ibid.

[22] Ibid., p.18.

[23] Ibid.

[24] Ibid., p.25.

[25] Ibid., p.31.

[26] Bid., p.32.

[27] Ibid., p.41.

[28] Ibid., p.47.

[29] Ibid., p.55.

[30] Ibid.

[31] Ibid., pp.65-66.

[32] Ibid., p.71.

[33] Ibid.

[34] Ibid., p.88.

[35] Ibid., pp.95-96.

[36] Ibid., p.101.

37 Ibid., p.113.

38 Ibid., p.172.

39 MAWA Foundation (3 January 2021). "Kebbi Lawmaker N41 Million Constituency Project, Scam Not Traceable To Any Location"> https://mawafd.org/kebbi-lawmaker-n41-million-constituency-project-scam-not-traceable-to-any-location/

40 BudgIT Tracka (June 2018-November 2019). 2018 Constituency Projects Tracking Report: Fighting for Communities Left Behind(Abridged Version), pp.14-15.

41 Ibid., p.16.

42 Ibid., p.19.

43 Ibid.

44 Ibid., p.45.

45 Ibid., p.46.

46 Ibid., p.49.

47 Ibid.

48 @TrackaNG posted on 20 February 2021 on Twitter

49 MAWA Foundation (14 March 2021). "Two Years After, Abaribe N30 Million Constituency Project Remains Abandoned" https://mawafd.org/two-years-after-abaribe-n30-mil-

lion-constituency-project-remains-abandoned/

[50] @TrackaNG posted on 28 January 2021 on Twitter

[51] @TrackaNG posted on 13 January 2021 on Twitter

[52] Ibid.

[53] Ibid.

[54] Ibid.

[55] @TrackaNG posted on 15 January 2021 on Twitter

[56] @TrackaNG posted on 17 February 2021 on Twitter

[57] @TrackaNG posted on 18 February 2021 on Twitter

[58] @TrackaNG posted in February 2021 on Twitter

[59] Ibid.

[60] @TrackaNG posted on 26 February 2021 on Twitter

[61] @TrackaNG posted on 19 March 2021 on Twitter

CHAPTER FIVE

[1] Developmentdiaries.com (19 October 2020) "Nigeria: Abandoned Projects and Tracka Advocacy">https://www.developmentdiaries.com/2020/10/nigeria-abandoned-projects-and-tracka-advocacy/

[2] Ibid.

[3] Iyatse, Geoff (24 February 2021). "FG Passes New N10 Trillion Debt To Unborn Nigerians" Guardian.ng>https://guardian.ng/news/fg-passes-new-n10-trillion-debt-to-unborn-nigerians/

[4] Olalekan, Fakoyejo (20 January 2020). "President Buhari Not To Blame For Increase In Debt – DMO DG" Nairametrics.com > https://nairametrics.com/2020/01/20/president-buhari-not-to-blame-for-increase-in-debt-dmo-dg/

[5] Hukoomi.gov.qa (Retrieved 28 March 2021) "Qatar National Vision 2030: Everything You Need to Know" > https://hukoomi.gov.qa/en/about-qatar/qatar-national-vision-2030

[6] Oxfordbusinessgroup.com (Retrieved 26 March 2021) "Infrastructure Building to Help Sustain Qatar's Growth Past 2022" > https://oxfordbusinessgroup.com/overview/infrastructure-building-help-sustain-qatars-growth-past-2022

[7] USAToday.com (Published 7 July 2019 Retrieved 29 March 2021). "These Are The 25 Richest Countries In The World" https://eu.usatoday.com/story/money/2019/07/07/richest-countries-in-the-world/39630693/

[8] Ibid.

[9] Arafat, Weal et al (2018) "Infrastructure Developing and Economic Growth in United Arab Emirates" in: Business and Economic Research (Vol. 8), p.96.

[10] Ibid., pp. 96,101 & 111.

[11] Al Maktoum, Mohammed bin Rashid (2018). "UAE Vision 2021" https://www.vision2021.ae/en/uae-vision

[12] National Committee on Sustainable Development Goals (2017). UAE And The 2030 Agenda For Sustainable Development Excellence In Implementation

[13] Yang, Gu Qing & R.N. Sugitha Nadarajah (2017). "A Visionary's Experience In Incorporating Infrastructure Into Long-Term Urban Planning - Interview With Dr. Liu Thai Ker" in: Journal of Infrastructure, Policy and Development (Vol. 1), pp.90-97.

[14] Ibid.

PROJECT MANAGEMENT AND POLITICS

EMBARKING ON A DANGEROUS CRITICAL PATH

Nigerian politicians are caught in an evil cycle, and the consequences are dire. The purpose of government should be to protect its people, but what is happening in a country where resources are so abundant, yet so wasted?

As a succession of elected leaders prioritize policies, projects, and programs solely on the basis of their own personal gain, they concurrently abandon what their predecessors began, frustrating potential and prosperity that should be widespread among Nigeria's people.

In this incisive look at years of corruption and project mismanagement, Dr. Darlington Akaiso clearly outlines the problems inherent in this vicious cycle. He takes us through a myriad of examples, then provides a glimmer of hope for a solutions-based response for a better Nigeria to come.

CPSIA information can be obtained
at www.ICGtesting.com
Printed in the USA
BVHW041302080721
611492BV00011B/212